Anonymous

Sacramento

The Commercial Metropolis of Northern and Central California

Anonymous

Sacramento
The Commercial Metropolis of Northern and Central California

ISBN/EAN: 9783337294137

Printed in Europe, USA, Canada, Australia, Japan

Cover: Foto ©Lupo / pixelio.de

More available books at **www.hansebooks.com**

SACRAMENTO

THE COMMERCIAL METROPOLIS OF NORTHERN AND CENTRAL CALIFORNIA

STATE CAPITOL AT SACRAMENTO.

1888.

SACRAMENTO,
A. J. JOHNSTON & CO.
PRINTERS & PUBLISHERS.

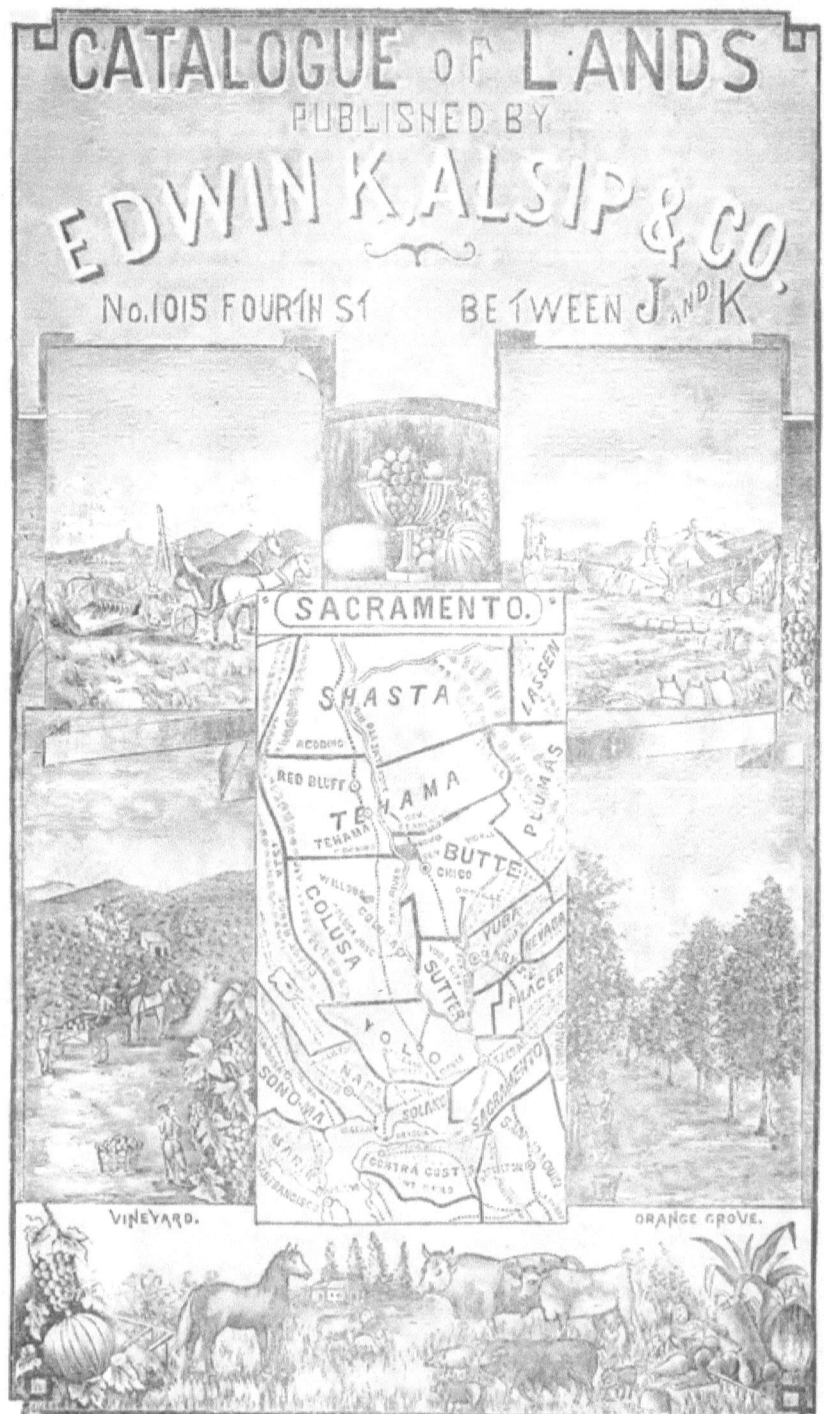

SACRAMENTO:

THE

Commercial Metropolis

OF

NORTHERN AND CENTRAL CALIFORNIA

SACRAMENTO:
A. J. JOHNSTON & CO., PUBLISHERS
1888

ALBION C. SWEETSER.   ED. F. AMSDEN.

SWEETSER & AMSDEN,

Real Estate and Insurance Agents.

REAL ESTATE BOUGHT AND SOLD ON COMMISSION.

OFFICE AND SALESROOM:

No. 1012 Fourth Street, between J and K Streets,

SACRAMENTO, CALIFORNIA.

MONEY LOANED ON REAL ESTATE

Having resided in Sacramento thirty-eight years, and had twenty-seven years experience in the Real Estate Business (nine years longer than any other real estate agent), we are prepared to give those seeking homes, or lands for investment, reliable information as to how and where to invest.

All grades of land for sale, in large or small tracts, some of which has produced four crops of alfalfa hay in a single year.

Also, *City Property*.

Particular attention given to the care of property for non-residents.

Send for Catalogues.

PREFACE.

Of the state of California and its resources, much of late years has been written and printed for dissemination among the people of the eastern states. Particularly has such information been published concerning the resources of the southern section of the state. As yet but little has been written of the central section—a vast, rich, but comparatively undeveloped territory—which in the very near future will as much astonish the world by the demonstration of its agricultural wealth, as did the state in 1849 by the richness of its gold mines.

In the pages following, nothing but facts, capable of absolute and satisfactory demonstration, are presented. Of the section of which this work treats, the facts furnish an ample and convincing argument of its resources and capabilities. It has been the endeavor of the writers—and they are gentlemen of state-wide reputation—to present but the actual facts.

The plan of this work, it will be observed, has been to present papers prepared by gentlemen who have special information on the subjects on which they treat. In some instances, two or more papers touch in a measure on the same subject, and it has been regarded that the reader will thus have the advantage of the views of the several writers on matters upon which accurate information is most desired.

LUDWIG MEBIUS.   P. C. DRESCHER.

MEBIUS & CO.

IMPORTERS

AND

Wholesale Grocers

WHOLESALE DEALERS IN

PROVISIONS,   TOBACCO,
CIGARS,   LIQUORS.

EXPORTERS OF CALIFORNIA HOPS

Corner of Front and K Streets,

SACRAMENTO,   CALIFORNIA.

Real Estate Salesrooms

No. 325 J Street, Sacramento, Cal.

All kinds of Farming Land for Sale, Improved and Unimproved.

Also, a Large List of City Property For Sale.

MONEY TO LOAN IN LARGE AND SMALL SUMS.

☞ Send for our List of Farms. ☜

CONTENTS.

1.—SACRAMENTO COUNTY. General Description of the County—Boundaries—Rivers—Facilities for Irrigation—Water and Rail Transportation Facilities—Unlimited Natural Water Power—Early History and Settlement—Soil Characteristics—Valuations of Land—Area of County—Profits from Small Holdings—Early Transcontinental Railroad History—Volume of Export Commerce—Railroad Shops—Roads and Bridges—County Public Buildings and Institutions—State Capitol and Grounds—State Printing Office—School Books Manufactured by the State—Exposition Pavilion and Stock Exhibition Grounds—County Statistics 1887—Property Valuation—Volume of Local Business—Churches—Education—Postal and Telegraphic Facilities—General Agricultural Resources—Towns. By WINFIELD J. DAVIS. 9

2.—SACRAMENTO CITY. General Description—Its Advantageous Position—Libraries—Schools—Art Gallery—Manufactories—Public Parks—Early History—Water Supply—Fire Protection—Open Air Concerts. By WINFIELD J. DAVIS. . 21

3.—AGRICULTURAL RESOURCES OF SACRAMENTO COUNTY. Soil and Climate—Winter Fruits: Oranges, Lemons, Pomegranates, Olives and Persimmons—Spring Fruits: Strawberries, Raspberries, Blackberries and Cherries—Early Summer Fruits: Peaches, Apricots, Pears and Plums—Fall Fruits: Apples, Pears, Grapes, Quinces, Prunes and Peaches—Fruit Drying and Canning—Sacramento as a Fruit Shipping Center—Volume of Fruit Shipments to the East—Hop Culture—Alfalfa—Beans—Figs—Nuts—Broom Corn—Vegetables. By P. E. PLATT. 26

4.—SOCIAL CONDITIONS IN SACRAMENTO. Character of our Population—Literary Tastes—Art Gallery and School—Public Charities—Religion—Education. By J. A. WOODSON. 37

5.—CLIMATE AND RAINFALL. Statistics of Temperature, Rainfall, and General Climatic Conditions—Comparisons with the Citrus and Olive Belt of Northern and Western Italy, and with the State of North Carolina. By JAS. A. BARWICK. 42

6.—SACRAMENTO A NATURAL TRADE CENTER. Railroad Shops—Flouring Mills—Manufactories Generally—Unlimited Natural Water Power—Transportation Facilities. By C. K. MCCLATCHY. 48

7.—SACRAMENTO AND ADJACENT COUNTIES. General Description—Irrigation Facilities—Hops—Alfalfa—Fruit and Berry Culture—Land Production—Bartlett Pears—Grapes—Raisins—The Tributary Counties—Land Valuations—Climate. By GEORGE W. HANCOCK. 51

8.—PRODUCE SHIPPED FROM SACRAMENTO CITY. Interesting statement by one who has spent years in purchasing, packing and shipping fruits and produce from Sacramento—Results of the observations of one of our practical merchants in that line—Natural Advantages—Transportation Facilities—General Agricultural Advantages—Volume of Fruit Shipments—The World for a Market—Dried and Canned Products—Vegetables. By EUGENE J. GREGORY. . . . 57

9.—THOROUGHBRED HORSES. Climatic Advantages—What we have produced in that line—Possibilities of the Future. By JOHN A. SHEEHAN. . . . 59

10.—EDUCATIONAL. Public and Private Schools of the City and County—Courses of Study—Cost of Maintenance—Statistical—Social and Fraternal Organizations. By ELWOOD BRUNER. 62

11.—SANITARY ASPECT OF SACRAMENTO. Location of Sacramento City—Sewage—Water Supply—Analysis of the Water Used—Climatology—Health—Death Rate. By JAMES H. PARKINSON, M. D. 65

ENDORSEMENT.

SACRAMENTO, December 30, 1887.

We have carefully examined the proof sheets of the articles published in this work, and from our personal knowledge of the writers and of the facts stated by them, we cordially endorse this volume as containing a fair and truthful statement of the resources of Sacramento county.

EUGENE J. GREGORY,
Mayor City of Sacramento.

F. F. TEBBETTS,
President Board of Supervisors Sacramento County.

Entered according to Act of Congress, in the year 1878, by A. J. JOHNSTON & Co., in the office of the Librarian of Congress, at Washington, D. C.

SACRAMENTO COUNTY.

By WINFIELD J. DAVIS, Official Reporter of the Courts.

GENERAL DESCRIPTION.

The county of Sacramento was organized by the first state legislature, and is the central county in the state. Within its confines was early located the seat of state government. The annual state fairs have been held in Sacramento city since the organization of the State Agricultural Society, and from that city was projected the first transcontinental railway on the American continent. The county of Sacramento is bounded on the north by the counties of Sutter and Placer, on the east by El Dorado and Amador, on the south by San Joaquin and Contra Costa, and on the west by Solano and Yolo. To those at all familiar with the resources of the state, it is readily apparent that Sacramento county is the very heart of the richest portion of Central California. Within its borders is situated the largest city in the interior of the state, the trade from which extends to the north, to the vast middle belt of the state and throughout the state of Nevada.

The Rivers.—Passing through the county from north to south is the Sacramento river, the largest watercourse in the state, and traversing it from east to west are the American, Cosumnes and Mokelumne rivers. The Sacramento is navigable from San Francisco bay far above the city of Sacramento, and even above the city of Colusa. Steamboats ply daily from Sacramento to San Francisco, and the extensive cereal products of the great counties of Butte, Colusa, Sutter, Yuba, Yolo and Sacramento are cheaply transported to the sea-board for foreign shipment on barges floated on the bosom of that magnificent stream. In the lower portion of the county the proprietors of the river bank orchards own and manage a line of steamboats on which their fruits are transported at a trifling cost to the San Francisco market or to Sacramento city for shipment to the east. In the cases of the American, Mokelumne and Cosumnes rivers, their availability and adaptability for purposes of irrigation is unequalled elsewhere in the state. Particularly is this the case with the American and Cosumnes, mountain streams, running through a country the topography of which peculiarly favors the diversion of their waters, not only for the purpose of irrigation, but for the purpose of affording power.

As early as 1840 Captain John A. Sutter, the pioneer settler in Central California, recognized the availability of the American river for purposes of irrigation and power, and had his plans not been thwarted by the discovery of the gold at Coloma, in January, 1848, and the consequent demoralization of agricultural and mechanical interests, he would have completed a race for the conveyance of water to irrigate his wheat fields, and to afford power for the running of his flouring and saw mills. What was then observed in the way of such advantages by that far-sighted and enterprising pioneer of those very early days has since been demonstrated with mathematical certainty by distinguished engineers employed by the state, and their reports to the legislature have shown that if the question of irrigating the lands of the county, of furnishing an inexhaustible power, or of supplying cities of unlimited population with water fresh and pure, shall ever arise in Sacramento county, it is one of very easy solution. However, except in the dry season of 1863—4, when the drought was general throughout the state, there has been no particular need for irrigation in the county, save in some fruit sections, remote from the rivers, where resort has successfully been made to wells, the water being raised by windmills and run in trenches over the land. In some sections of the state water courses are rare, and in those that exist water flows only during the wet season. When most needed—in the summer and fall—the streams dry out, or flow but an inconsiderable quantity of water. In the sections south in the state, where agriculture and fruit-raising cannot be successfully carried on without irrigation, the natural scarcity of water has given rise to protracted and bitter litigation, and the legislature of the state was in 1886 called in extra session for the purpose of formulating laws for the regulation of the diversion of waters from streams in those sections. That question never has been and never will be important in the county of Sacramento. With four never-failing rivers traversing it, with the demonstration that artesian water is within easy reach, and with the result of years of practical experience that with the major portion of our land irrigation is not needed, the question of water is one that has not and never will have to be considered with seriousness.

The Soil.—The land of Sacramento county is of three characters —foothill, plains and river bottom. The foothill land is peculiarly adapted to the production of fruits and grapes. The Natoma vineyard, near Folsom, is one of the largest in the world, and the properties of the company rank with the most profitable in the state, so far as production per acre is concerned. Very many acres of land, of equal value for production, remain unimproved and are held at comparatively insignificant valuations. They but await the application of enterprising labor to render them principalities to their possessors. But a few years ago the foothill lands of California were regarded by our own people as almost valueless, but the successes in fruit and vinegrowing on that character of lands along the line of the Central Pacific railroad, in the adjoining county of Placer, and the peculiar adaptability of the produce for long shipment, gave immediate value to them, and to-day lands are held there at $100 per acre and upwards, which ten years ago could not be sold for $1.25. Equally good land of that character is abundant in the county of Sacramento, and can be purchased cheaply.

The plains lands are mainly devoted to grain raising, and there have been no crop failures with them since the American occupation of the country. On this character of land where the vine has been planted it has flourished without irrigation. In some portions of the county—notably Florin—fruits, berries and grapes are extensively produced on this class of land, and from small holdings munificent incomes are derived. In many cases, however, the land thereabouts is irrigated by artesian water pumped by windmills.

The best lands, however, are those on the immediate banks of the rivers. Those lands are devoted to the production of fruits and vegetables, and the income per acre—particularly from the lands on the Sacramento river is fabulous. Their fortunate owners reside in costly houses, the architectural designing of which equals that of the homes of the wealthy in the larger cities, and at the end of the fruit season their settlements with their agents at Sacramento and San Francisco leave a respectable fortune to each landowner.

The area of Sacramento county is 620,000 acres, and it has 968 plus square miles of territory. Hardly a foot of its land is not susceptible of successful cultivation, and the major part of it will favorably rank with the best land in the Union. Before the American rule, and under Spanish and Mexican dominion, the choicest sections of the territory now constituting the state of California were granted away in large tracts to individuals. Upon the acquisition of the country by the Americans, a land commission was established, and many of these vast grants were confirmed to those who had received the favorable consideration of the Mexican government. United States patents were issued, and with the development of our agricultural resources, the people of the new state were confronted with the same problem which had created the anti-rent troubles in the state of New York—the aggregation of large tracts of valuable lands in the hands of the few. Fortunately, however, from the then speculative disposition of our people, the evils which flowed from that landed monopoly in New York were here averted, and the necessities of the grant owners compelled the cutting up and sale of their estates. At the organization of the state government, the county of Sacramento embraced no less than five large land grants. To-day but one remains intact, and its owners have signified their willingness to subdivide it on reasonable terms.

Railroad Facilities.—The city of Sacramento is entitled to the credit of being the initial point in the construction of the first great transcontinental railroad. When the discovery of the gold mines was made in 1848, and the news of the marvelous wealth of the placers reached the eastern states and Europe, a tide of immigration flowed into the new state unprecedented at any other time in the history of the world. Separated from the other states by an expanse of three thousand miles of uninhabited territory, by deserts and mountain barriers, and approached by sea only after a voyage of months on tempestuous oceans, the necessity for railroad connection with the elder states to the east was early suggested. The first political meeting held in the new state passed resolutions strongly urging on the federal government immediate action looking to the construction of a railroad across the continent. By many the intervening mountain ranges—the Sierra Nevadas and the Rockies—were regarded as insurmountable, and it was believed that human skill could not successfully carry a railroad over them. In 1854-5, surveys for a route were made under the direction of the secretary of war, but the reports submitted by the able engineers who conducted the explorations were generally unfavorable to the successful accomplishment of the great enterprise. Finally, in the early part of the administration of President Lincoln, Congress passed the "Pacific Railroad Bill," authorizing the construction of the road, and granting aid to those who might engage in the enterprise. While the press and people of the state unanimously favored the prosecution and successful culmination of the work, after the bill had been passed, capital held back and manifested a very decided unwillingness to embark in a venture the outcome of which was regarded as hazardous. However, an organization was effected at Sacramento by Stanford, the Crockers, Hopkins and Huntington —men engaged in merchandising in the city—and after having failed in the effort to raise money by subscriptions from capitalists to the capital stock of the company, they decided to take hold of the project almost alone, and to stake their private fortunes in the result. On January 8, 1863, ground was broken for the construction of the first overland railroad on the American continents at Front and K streets in Sacramento city, the first shovelful of earth being moved by the then governor, Leland Stanford. Work was prosecuted steadily thereafter, and on May 10, 1869, the last spike in the completion of the work was driven by the same gentleman who had performed the initial act six years before. The years that have since passed have been marked by other grand works in the line of internal improvements; but prosecuted at that particular time, when the country was embroiled in civil war, when money was scarce, and when public judgment was largely against the feasibility and practicability of the enterprise, its successful accomplishment is certainly a matter of pardonable congratulation to the people of the city and county among whom the men who embarked in the enterprise resided.

Few counties in California contain a greater mileage of railroads than Sacramento. From the capital city the Central Pacific leads eastward across the continent; the California and Oregon passes to the north into Oregon and from thence to the eastern states; the Western Pacific, which terminates at Oakland, but which connects with the Southern overland railroad line, and from it at the flourishing town of Galt branches off a line running up into the rich county of Amador; the California Pacific connecting it in almost an air line with San Francisco; and the Sacramento valley, which extends into the princely county of El Dorado. From most all of these roads branches extend into the various counties of Central California. From its geographical position Sacramento city is the natural railroad center of the central and upper portions of the state, and the agricultural and mineral products of this great and rich section of the American Union are shipped from her ample storehouses. To give something of an idea of the export commerce from the city, we quote the following from the San Francisco Chronicle of November 15, 1887:

"More freight was sent east from Sacramento during October than from any other city in the state except San Francisco. The shipments were as follows: Beans, 22,350 pounds; books and stationery, 1190; brandy, 38,510; canned goods, 753,870; dried fruit, 919,780; green fruit, 3,447,840; glue, 1600; hides, 81,160; honey, 37,450; hops, 757,190; leather, 6250; machinery, 20,030; miscellaneous, 21,890; nuts, 50,440; potatoes, 72,620; raisins, 2,177,350; canned salmon, 71,580; wine, 816,910; wool, greasy, 41,860; wool, pulled, 83,080; woolen goods, 4040; total, 8,927,490. The other railroad shipping points sent East during the same time the following amounts: San Francisco, 9,101,530; Oakland, 2,675,-090; Los Angeles, 2,483,210; Colton, 385,280; San Jose, 7,326,-500; Stockton, 336,910; Marysville, 906,010."

The shipments of fruits from the city of Sacramento largely exceed those from other shipping points in the state. The depot building at the foot of H street is one of the most attractive and expensive in the United States. Connected with it and a part of the immense structure is a complete hotel. Through the depot 54 trains pass each day. Near by are the shops of the Southern Pacific railroad company, reference to the extent of which and the number of men employed is made elsewhere in this volume.

Roads and Bridges.—No county in the state has better roads than Sacramento. One can drive to any part of the county at any time of the year with no inconvenience, and over roads that favorably compare with the streets in very many towns elsewhere in the state. All of the bridges on public highways are the property of the county, and with the roads are free for travel.

County Public Buildings and Institutions.—The court-house, formerly the state capitol, is a substantial and imposing structure It affords ample accommodations for the offices of the various county officers and the county judiciary. On the same lot has been erected the hall of records, a brick and iron building, thoroughly fire proof, in which the public record books are kept. In no other county in the State are the records so secure from fire. The building contains no combustible material save the meager shelving. Even the laths for the retention of the plastering are of iron. Two miles from the city is located the county hospital and farm. The building, standing in the midst of a vast, fertile and highly cultivated tract of land, is built on the pavilion plan, the wings radiating from the main building as do the fingers from the hand. Not only are the indigent sick humanely provided for, but the aged poor find there a haven of rest in which they can pass the evening of their lives in happiness.

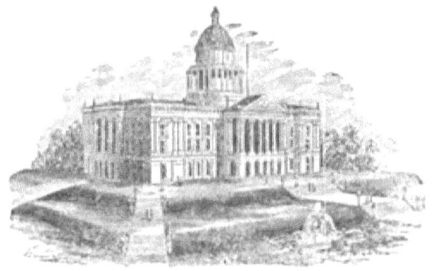

The State Capitol and Grounds.—The grounds of the state, on which stand the public buildings, comprise ten blocks in the heart of Sacramento city. The state capitol is located at the intersection of M and Eleventh streets, in the western end of the state park. Within this building are the offices of the various state departments, and the magnificent state library. The legislative halls occupy a portion of the second floor. To the eastward in the park is the state printing office—one of the most complete public printing establishments in the world. It is owned and controlled by the state, and all the public printing is there done. In the third story is an electrotyping department and book bindery. In 1884 a constitutional amendment was approved by the people providing for the compilation and printing of all school text-books by the state; and in this printing office the work of composition, engraving, electrotyping, printing and binding on the state series of text-books for the public schools is performed. The books are furnished to the people of the state at the actual cost of production, leaving out of consideration the expenditure for the plant. As a result, in this state, we will soon have a uniform series of school books which will be furnished to the people at a nominal price.

To the south of the state printing office stands the exposition building of the State Agricultural Society. While one of the largest structures on the continent erected for that purpose, it has proved too limited in capacity to contain the exhibits sent to the annual fairs held in the city; and, while it has had to be enlarged, more space is demanded, and the board of directors have in contemplation the extension of its wings, with the view of adding to the capacity of the building, without marring its architectural appearance.

The stock exhibition grounds and race track of the State Agricultural Society are in the eastern portion of the city. This park is one of the largest of the kind in the state. The race track is said to be the speediest in the United States, but however that may be, it is certain that some of the most noted horses in the world made their records within the confines of the park at Sacramento. The grand stands have a capacity of accommodating 10,000 people; and at the annual exhibitions of fine stock and the races the attendance from the city and abroad in the state is so large as to crowd.

County Statistics, 1887.—From the official report of County Assessor A. L. Frost, made to the State authorities, the following figures are taken:

NUMBER OF ACRES SOWN FOR CROP OF 1887.

Of wheat	74,385
Of oats	427
Of barley	38,740
Of corn	5,428
Of hay	39,185
Number of fruit trees growing	484,045
Number of acres of grape vines growing	64,65
Number of grape vines growing	4,525,500
Number of acres in table grapes	1,445
Number of acres in wine grapes	3,020

Total assessed valuation of property in county, $29,634,995.50.

Under the provisions of the state constitution the assessment is based on the valuations on the first Monday in March immediately preceding. Owing to the well known fact that owners of property universally underestimate their wealth to assessors, it is fair to assume that the above sum is not above two-thirds of the actual valuation on the day named. Since then a very decided increase of real estate values has occurred all over the county, and it is estimated that the assessed valuation in 1888 will be not less than $35,000,000. The agricultural statistics are also low, for the same reason that the valuation is short.

Volume of Local Business.—The following table, furnished by P. F. Dolan, collector of county licenses, is illustrative of the volume of the local business of the county:

Wholesale groceries	21	Lumber yards	10
Retail groceries	183	Lumber, hardwood	3
Wholesale hardware	5	Oil stores, wholesale	3
Retail hardware	23	Livery stables	19
Wholesale agricultural implements	9	Gun stores	4
Retail agricultural implements	15	Liquor stores, wholesale	6
Drug stores, wholesale	6	Variety stores	31
Drug stores, retail	22	Paint and glass, wholesale and retail	5
Clothing stores, wholesale	5	Furniture stores	13
Clothing stores, retail	39	Furnishing stores	4
Wood and coal yards	11	Confectioners stores	9
Carriages, wholesale	7	General findings stores	3
Wire stores, wholesale	4	Tobacco stores, wholesale	7
Wire stores, retail	9	Tobacco stores, retail	19
Stove stores, wholesale	5	Paper and books, wholesale	3
Stove stores, retail	18	Paper and books, retail	9
Gas fixtures, wholesale	3	Fruit stores, wholesale	8
Gas fixtures, retail	9	Fruit stores, retail	37
Willowware, wholesale	2	Seeds, retail and wholesale	5
Willowware, retail	7	Optical institutions	3
Jewelry stores	18	Feed stores	17
Hat stores, wholesale	3	Sewing machine stores	5
Hat stores, retail	11	Harness stores	9
Wall paper, wholesale	3	Harness stores, wholesale	3
Wall paper, retail	9	Crockery and glass stores	9
Carpet stores	19	Piano stores	4
Dry goods, wholesale	5	Produce stores	17
Dry goods, retail	27	Iron stores	5
Fancy stores	16	Music stores	4
Millinery stores	19	Books, wholesale and retail	7
Shoe stores, wholesale	3	Wineries	2
Shoe stores, retail	27	Flour mills	5
Coffee and spice, wholesale	2	Hide stores	3
Coffee, tea, spice, retail	7	Carriage and wagon manufactories	15
Tea, wholesale and retail	3		

Churches.—Freedom of religious opinion—as guaranteed by the Federal Constitution—is nowhere in the Union more respected than in the State of California. Its population was drawn originally, after the discovery of the gold mines in 1848, from all portions of the Union. In the early days the cost of passage to a country then so remote kept back the scruff, and only those of sufficient means

CATHOLIC CATHEDRAL, SACRAMENTO.

dared to undertake the journey. The result was that our early American population comprised the cream of the society of America and Europe. Many have since died, but their descendants, native born in the state, inherit their characteristics, and are now prominently in the front in developing the unlimited resources of the great commonwealth which their fathers in their early manhood won for the American Union. At no time in the history of the State, since the American occupancy, did religion not have a firm foothold, and as towns and cities grew up, the spires of churches were raised in them. Every denomination has its houses of worship, and in each city and town in the county the Sabbath is observed, and laying aside the business affairs of life, the people gather in their houses of worship and render appropriate homage to the Supreme Ruler of the Universe. The subjects of education and fraternal societies are fully treated of in a special article in this volume, written by Hon. Elwood Bruner.

Postoffices.—Recently an appropriation was made by the federal congress of $100,000 for the purchase of a site and the erection of a postoffice building in the city of Sacramento. Such a structure has long been needed. Outside of the city of San Francisco no postoffice in the state does a larger volume of business than that at Sacramento. In the numerous towns in the county the postal service is complete, and the promptness of mail delivery is unsurpassed elsewhere in the union. Telegraphic communication also extends to every town in the county.

General Agricultural Resources.—For many years California was regarded as valueless save for its mineral wealth, but it was not long before American enterprise saw that its richness in the line of agriculture and fruit-raising was incomparable with any other portion of the world. Gradually experimental plantings were made, and with the advance of time the successes met with induced a widening of the field, and the permanency of the industry was established. From the cultivation of cereals, the step was taken successfully in the line of fruit and vine raising, and lastly in the growing of oranges and lemons. At the date at which we now write (November, 1887,) the oranges and lemons on the many trees in Sacramento county are ripening, and in a short time will be in the market. As illustrating the character of the climate we have here, we will state that at a recent fair there was exhibited a banana tree with its fruit on it, which had been grown in the open air in a yard in the city. The date palm and other tropical vegetation thrive in our door yards, and the luxuriance of the growth of vegetation generally is a matter of astonishment to those who visit among us.

The river bottom lands in the county have been found to be peculiarly adapted to the production of hops, and no county in the state produces as great a quantity of that commodity as Sacramento. In late years, the prices of that product in the markets of the world has been unprecedentedly high, and the fortunate producers have realized fortunes from the sale of their crops. This condition of things was brought about by the failure of the hop crops elsewhere in the world, and the producers in the state of California practically monopolized the markets and dictated the prices.

The Towns.—To the city of Sacramento particular reference is made in a special article in this volume. Of the towns in the county, aside from the principal city, Galt is the largest. Situated in the heart of a rich agricultural section, and midway between the cities of Sacramento and Stockton in the county of San Joaquin, with direct rail communication to the principal cities in the state and the terminus of a railroad tapping the rich county of Amador, it enjoys a position of advantage almost unequalled in the state by an interior town. Its business blocks are built of brick, and the residence portion of the town contains many models of the perfection in architecture.

Folsom, on the line of the Sacramento and Placerville railroad, was formerly a mining town, but the country surrounding it is now mainly employed for the production of fruits and vines.

Numerous smaller towns dot the county, in each of which business is prosperous.

THE CITY OF SACRAMENTO.

By WINFIELD J. DAVIS, Official Reporter of the Courts.

The great seal of the state of California is happily designed. The goddess Minerva is the principal feature. Minerva, the happiest of conceptions of Grecian mythology, sprang forth fully armored and with a mighty war shout from the brain of Jupiter. She was the patron of heroism among men, the protectress of the arts of peace, the symbol of thought and the goddess of wisdom. So did California come into the sisterhood of the states of the American Union full fledged, and without territorial probation. Like Minerva, when the hour of trouble came, she was the patron of heroism. From her soil was taken the gold, without which the confederacy of the states could not have been maintained.

The capital city of this great western state was happily located. Planted at the confluence of two large rivers, at the median between the great metropolis at the sea and the mines, it was a natural center. The era of mining passed, yet Sacramento found herself the heart of the richest agricultural section in the world. With the remarkable developments in the way of material resources that have been made in Northern and Central California in the last few years, Sacramento has kept full pace. To her mart the products of the great commonwealth naturally drift, and are shipped to the outside world. No city in the state or nation has a more advantageous position and surrounding.

The city of Sacramento is the county seat of Sacramento county and capital of California. Latitude 38° 35″ N., longitude 121° 30″ W. Distance by rail from San Francisco eighty-three miles. The city is located on an extensive plain, on the east bank of the Sacramento river, immediately south of its confluence with the American river.

The streets are wide and cross at right angles; those running east and west are designated by the letters of the alphabet, and those crossing them, north and south, are numbered, commencing at the Sacramento river. The business portion is built of brick, and the residence portion of wood. Shade trees are abundant, and almost every residence yard is lawned and planted with orange trees, palms and ornamental plants. The climate is semi-tropical, and in the

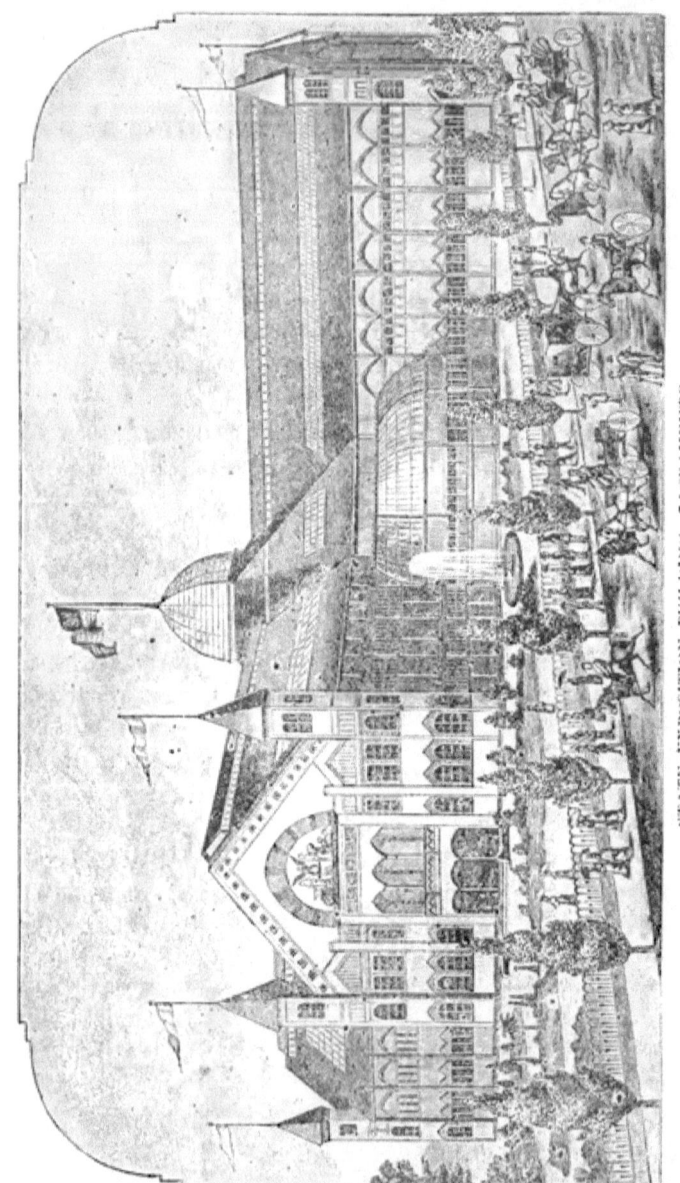

STATE EXPOSITION BUILDING, SACRAMENTO.

open air the year around there is a luxuriant growth of trees and flowers.

The first railroad in California, extending from Sacramento into El Dorado county, was formally opened on February 22d, 1856. Work on the Central Pacific railroad was inaugurated at Sacramento January 8th, 1863, and the last spike was driven May 10th, 1869. Sacramento is on the line of the California and Oregon, Western Pacific, Central Pacific, California Pacific, and Sacramento and Placerville railroads. All these roads are of the Southern Pacific System, the shops of which are located in the city, covering twenty-five acres of land, and furnishing constant employment to about 2,000 men. The company's hospital is also located in the city. A line of steamboats run to San Francisco on the Sacramento river and the bays, and another as far up the same stream as Red Bluff. The Sacramento river is spanned opposite the city by a railroad and wagon bridge, connecting it with the town of Washington, Yolo county; and the American river is bridged on the line of Twelfth street, and also by a railroad bridge a short distance above. All the bridges in the county and all roads are free.

The capital of California was permanently located at Sacramento February 25th, 1854, and in 1869 the present capitol building was completed at a cost of about $3,000,000. The building is the finest in the state. In the capitol park are also the exposition pavilion of the State Agricultural Society, and the state printing office, in which are printed, in addition to the usual work for the state, the text-books for use in the public schools. The State Agricultural Society has also an extensive park for the exhibition of stock, and one of the finest race tracks in the world. The state fairs are annually held in September. The masons and odd fellows have each imposing temples, in which their lodge-rooms are located. The United States government has purchased a site for a postoffice building, to be erected immediately, for which an appropriation of $100,000 has been made. The county court-house (formerly used for a state capitol) cost $200,000; and a brick and iron hall of records has recently been completed at a cost of $50,000. The county hospital, built on the pavilion plan, can accommodate one hundred and seventy-five patients, and cost $75,000.

There are in the city twenty-seven hotels, one national and three commercial and savings banks, three daily, two semi-weekly (German), four weekly newspapers, and three monthlies, and seventeen churches. The catholic cathedral, now in course of erection, will cost $250,000. There are also twelve public school buildings, three colleges, four private schools, and one art school.

The state library contains some sixty thousand volumes; and the free public library, of twelve thousand volumes, is maintained by a small city tax, and with the two-story building in which it is contained, is the property of the city. The order of odd fellows maintain a library of about eight thousand volumes. The Crocker art gallery is also the property of the city. It is a brick and iron building, three stories high, and in it are contained some of the finest paintings and statuary in the union, together with an extensive cabinet of minerals, the property of the State.

The city has four flouring mills, four planing mills, two box factories, one broom factory, one cannery, two wineries, seven carriage manufactories, two spice mills, three potteries, and five foundries.

Sacramento is lighted with gas and electricity, most of the street lighting being furnished by the latter means. The water works is the property of the city, and the water takers are charged at a rate to afford a revenue slightly in excess of the amount necessary to meet the running expenses of the works. The water is pumped directly into the city mains from the Sacramento river. The pumps are of the latest pattern, and the pressure is exerted by their power.

The state capitol park embraces twenty-five acres of land, and the city plaza two and a half. Both parks are lawned and planted with the choicest varieties of trees, shrubs and flowering and ornamental plants, and fountains are appropriately placed. During the summer months semi-weekly open-air concerts are given at these parks by brass bands, and are universally attended.

In 1839 Captain John A. Sutter established a fort, now included within the city limits, but the city was not laid out until 1848, after the discovery of gold. The thousands of gold seekers who arrived in the country came up the river to Sacramento in steamers and sailing vessels, and from that point proceeded by land to the mines. A canvas town was at first established on the river bank, and soon the substantial buildings of a city were erected. With the run of California cities, Sacramento has experienced its great fires. On November 2d, 1852, most of the business portion was burned, and again on July 13th, 1854, a great fire swept over the same ground and destroyed all that had been rebuilt after the 1852 conflagration. The city is now protected by an efficient paid fire department.

The city was incorporated by an act of the first legislature passed on February 27th, 1850; on April 24th, 1858, the governments of the city and county were consolidated; and on April 25th, 1863, the present charter, providing for a city government only, was passed.

Sacramento city is located in the heart of the richest agricultural section of California, having adjacent to it the counties of Yolo, Solano, Colusa, Butte, Placer, El Dorado, San Joaquin, Amador, and its own (Sacramento), in all of which, within the last few years, the increased value of lands has been marked; and notably in the foothill counties it has been discovered that their soils are peculiarly adapted to the production of grapes and citrus fruits. Lands in the foothills, which a few years ago were regarded as comparatively valueless, are now eagerly sought after at high prices. Cereals, fruits and hops are extensively grown in this section of the state, and the rearing of fine stock has of late years been made a specialty.

COUNTY COURT-HOUSE, SACRAMENTO.

THE AGRICULTURAL RESOURCES OF SACRAMENTO COUNTY.

By P. E. PLATT, of the fruit shipping firm of W. R. Strong & Co.

There is no spot on earth where fruit culture can be carried on more profitably, where greater variety can be produced, or where crops are surer than in that portion of the great Sacramento valley occupied by the county of Sacramento. At least this is the candid opinion of the writer who, after having spent fifteen years in the growing, packing and shipping of fruits to all the prominent cities of the east from Sacramento city, claims to know whereof he speaks, and will endeavor to convince the reader of the truth of the broad assertions herein made. This he thinks can be done best by a simple recital of facts, which can easily be verified, and which speak for themselves.

Soil and Climate.—There are three principal qualities of land in this county; the river bottom land, a deep, rich sediment deposit; a second bottom, which is a deep, sandy loam; and the red bedrock land of the plains; all of which are especially adapted to fruit of some kinds. It would be very difficult to name any product of the vegetable kingdom that could not be grown without irrigation on the rich river bottoms first mentioned, or with irrigation on the second named—while the red lands, owing to their shallowness, are not so desirable for tree culture; but berries of all kinds and every known variety of the finest table grapes do remarkably well on them. As the term is understood in the east, there is no winter here. The tender calla lily, as well as the olive, lemon and orange tree, blossom or bears fruit in the open air during the so called winter months. Neither is the heat of summer oppressive. There are no sunstrokes; and the farmer finds no inconvenience by reason of excessive heat. This article is not intended as a treatise on climatology, and the subject is mentioned only for the purpose of showing why the fruit grower here has no waste time, but can, if he will, utilize every day of the year; not only so, but he may actually gather fruit of some kind from his orchards, if not every day, certainly every month of the year. Let us contemplate for a moment the various crops that are now being successfully and extensively grown, and we will take them in order, commencing with the—

Winter Fruits.—These embrace oranges, lemons, pomegranates, olives and persimmons, which all ripen during the months of November, December and January. It has only been during the last four years that it has been generally known, even to our own residents, that the first two would do well here, consequently there are not a large number of bearing orchards to be found, but enough full grown trees exist to prove that they can and do thrive and produce fine fruit. The writer is personally connected with a firm that has brought to Sacramento county during the last three years over 50,000 orange and lemon trees, and will bring here, in addition to those now growing in its own nursery grounds this winter, at least 50,000 more. So great has been the demand for planting in this district, that it is sure that in a few years orange and lemon culture will form an important part of our industry. The crop of oranges in Sacramento county this year is estimated at 1,000 boxes. Five years hence it may be 50,000 boxes, and increase thereafter in like proportion. Oranges and lemons ripen here much earlier than in the southern part of the State. This fact may seem strange to many, but any who doubt it may prove it to their satisfaction very easily by comparing the fruit from the two localities in November. It is a fact that the oranges of Sacramento and other central counties are always sold at fancy prices long before any are received from the southern counties. This is an advantage which will be apparent at a glance. As to the quality: the writer, with others, in charge of the citrus fair exhibit from Central California at Chicago in the winter of 1886-7, was assured by experts that no better oranges ever reached that market. They were compared with the products of Florida, Louisiana and the Mediterranean, and suffered nothing by the comparison. The Japanese persimmon is the finest fruit of that family in the world, and grows here to the size of apples. Olives do well, and are being extensively planted. They are very profitable both for pickling and for oil. A grand opportunity is here presented for any one who will make a study of the business of raising olives, and who understands their commercial value. Samples of olive oil made in Sacramento county, and in the foothill region adjoining, were exhibited last year at Chicago, and were pronounced much superior to the imported article. The olive tree grows rapidly and bears prolifically; it is easily grown and very long lived. There can be no doubt that before many years the olives of California, like her raisins now are doing, will drive the foreign article out of the market. Olive culture, as well as orange and fig growing, is soon to be a leading industry in Sacramento county.

Spring Fruits.—We next come to the spring fruits, such as mature and are marketed in April, May and June. These embrace strawberries, raspberries, blackberries and cherries. Every acre of tillable land in Sacramento county will grow the finest strawberries in great profusion. This is a very profitable crop, and should be more largely cultivated. On the second year after the vines are set out a heavy crop may be gathered; and the fact that such quick results may be had makes it a desirable crop. Less than 500 acres are now cultivated in strawberries, whereas there is a market for the product of 10,000 acres at fairly remunerative prices. Raspberries do well here, as experiment has shown, and pay well. Blackberries are not so profitable, still they can be dried as well as sold green, and will pay, while cherries have always made the grower splendid returns. This latter variety grows to the largest size here, and as it is early and yields immense crops our fruit growers have no cause to regret having planted cherry trees. The only wonder is that there are not more of them. Doubtless there soon will be, as there seems to be no danger of over-production of cherries, for the reason that there are so many avenues through which they may be disposed of. First, coming in early they find a good local market both in Sacramento and San Francisco at good prices; secondly, they are of the finest quality for shipping, and many tons of them are sent out of the state daily during the season; and thirdly, the canneries will take all of certain varieties that can be grown.

Early Summer Fruits.—As he finishes picking his early fruits and collects the money for them, the Sacramento fruit grower finds he must keep right on with his early summer fruits, such as apricots, plums, peaches, pears and nectarines.

The first peaches are ready by the last of May or the first of June. Apricots and the early varieties of plums about the same time; and it is now that the fruit crop proper is reached, and from May to October there is no cessation in fruit picking, packing and shipping. To mention all the varieties of the above named species that are grown in this county, would require as much space as it is intended to devote to this entire article. So in passing we will simply draw attention to a few leading points. Peaches are very largely cultivated all over the county, but they reach their greatest importance on the bottom lands, along the banks of the American, Cosumnes and Sacramento rivers. From these districts alone hundreds of tons of fine, large, luscious peaches are marketed every day during the season. When the picking reaches its height, no doubt as many as 300 tons daily find a market; but this heavy supply only lasts a very few days.

Apricots ripen early, and while a limited quantity are shipped in a green state, the great bulk of this crop is either dried or preserved in cans, for both of which purposes it is unexcelled by any other fruit. Of all countries in the world California is the only one that has made a thorough success of the apricot. This seems to be its natural home, and in Sacramento county it reaches its very finest development in size, flavor and productiveness. With the entire world for a market, apricot growing cannot fail to become a leading and profitable industry.

Pears are also a leading summer fruit. A large number of varieties are grown, among which may be named the Madeline, Bloodgood, Dearborn Seedling, Le Count, Beurre Hardy, Seckel, Beurre Clargeau, B. Bose, Winter Nellis, etc., but chief among all is the world renowned California Bartlett pear. This pear has been shipped in great quantities from Sacramento city to every city of any size in the United States, and is as well known in New York, New Orleans, Chicago and Minneapolis as in San Francisco, or nearly so; hence a description of it here is unnecessary. Suffice it to say that it embraces all the fine qualities that can be named in a pear. It grows on the rich lands of the Sacramento river in larger quantities and size than any where else in the world. Needless to say it has always been profitable in Sacramento county. The writer knows of instances where an acre of Bartlett pear trees have never failed during the last ten years to yield a net income of over $500 per annum, and often as high as $800 or $1,000. These orchards are within a mile or two of Sacramento city, and can easily be found.

Plums are also very profitable. They grow to a large size, and as they keep well when properly handled, they are shipped in vast quantities to the eastern markets every year. There are none like them in quality of size and flavor. Besides being shipped green, they are sold to canners in large lots and are dried in the sun, and sell well in this way.

Early in the summer also apples of various kinds are shipped from

SENATOR ROUTIER'S VINEYARD AND ORCHARD, ROUTIER'S STATION, SACRAMENTO COUNTY.

Sacramento to the states and territories west of the Missouri. Apple culture has been neglected, but certain varieties are very profitable, and should be more extensively cultivated. Nectarines do well, but are not considered as profitable as other fruits.

Fall Fruits.—In the fall fruits we have apples, pears, grapes, quinces, prunes, and peaches. Of these we will refer to only two: grapes and prunes, the others having been already mentioned.

Sacramento county is pre-eminently the home of the grape. While it is true that grapes do well all over the northern and central part of California, yet it cannot be denied that on the red lands of the Sacramento plains they reach their highest perfection. The table varieties include the Flaming Tokay, the Muscat, Black Prince, Morocco, Emperor, Cornischon, and some others have always brought good prices for shipment to the east. These grapes are profitable at $15 to $20 per ton, but have usually sold at from $40 to $60 per ton.

French or petite prunes are becoming a leading fruit. They are remarkably prolific, and when cured, far excel in quality the imported article and bring much higher prices. While German prunes are being sold in New York at 5 and 6 cents per pound, our Sacramento grown French prunes readily bring 10 and 12 cents per pound here for shipment east. The culture of the prune is simple. They do well in any land that is suited for plums, and there is no difficulty whatever to cure and prepare them for market. Fortunes can be made in this fruit beyond doubt. Raisins are easily cured here, the weather being very favorable, and no rains ever interfere with the drying process.

Sacramento as a Fruit Shipping Center.—We now reach an important feature in the fruit industry of Sacramento county, and one to which particular attention should be drawn. It may not be generally known, but it is a fact that nearly ninety per cent. of the green fruit (other than oranges) that leaves the state of California for the eastern states and territories is shipped from Sacramento. It is true that other adjacent fruit districts supply some of this fruit, but it is shipped into Sacramento as the natural center, and here billed out to eastern points. The quantity grown in Sacramento county is large itself, and when there is added to this the product of El Dorado, Placer, Yolo, Solano, and other counties, the aggregate becomes something immense. To move the vast quantity of fruit, entire trains of ten to twelve, and sometimes more, cars each are chartered and run almost daily during the rush of the business. These trains are run east on passenger train time, and at low rates of freight—still better rates being expected soon.

Besides these special fruit trains many car loads are dispatched daily on passenger and freight trains, and the fruits of central California are now, as before stated, almost as well known in all the cities of the east as in Sacramento.

During the season just closing (October, 1887,) nearly 3,000 car loads of fruits and vegetables have been shipped from Sacramento to eastern trade centers, and when this quantity is added to the immense amount consumed by local and San Francisco canneries, an idea may be had of the vast yield of the district tributary to Sacramento.

The fruit shipping industry is yet in its infancy, but may now be considered as in a healthy condition, and bound to grow to gigantic proportions. As new railroads center here and fresh competition is added in the carrying trade, better facilities are afforded, quicker time, and lower rates, the business will be found practically to have no limit; but, of course, much has yet to be learned and many improvements can easily be made.

As showing the importance to which the fruit shipping business of Sacramento has grown, the following, taken from the Chicago Inter-Ocean of October 25, 1887, is not out of place:

"Sacramento has become the great fruit-shipping center of the state for the eastern markets, as the official figures abundantly demonstrate. During the year 1886 Sacramento shipped east in green fruit, twenty-six times as much as Los Angeles and San Francisco combined, and about nine-tenths of the entire amount of California fruit shipped. The figures from the railroad companies' books show that San Francisco shipped 525,290 pounds; Los Angeles, 201,960 pounds; Sacramento, 19,440,180 pounds, which is certainly a substantial showing   *   *   *   *   A good idea of the volume of the city's export business may be gained from the official figures of the Southern Pacific Company, which show that of the total of 51,589,820 pounds of freight shipped over that road from the entire state during August of the present year, Sacramento shipped about one-fourth.

"Sacramento is and will continue to be the chief fruit-exporting market of the state. Its advantages in this particular are so pronounced and so firmly established, that the city can afford to ignore the claims and misrepresentations of all envious rivals."

The fruit shipped in 1887 will greatly exceed in bulk the shipments of 1886.

It may not be thought out of place here to enumerate other productions that are being found highly profitable in this county, as well as some that are just passing the experimental stage.

The Hop Culture.—The following from the pen of Mr. Daniel Flint, a leading hop grower of Sacramento, will be of interest:

"Hop culture on this coast dates back to about 1858. Prior to that date most of the hops consumed came around Cape Horn, sealed up in tin cases. The first roots were imported by Wilson Flint, from Vermont, via the Isthmus. Hop culture developed very slowly, on account of the prejudice of the brewers against a hop that contained a much larger percentage of strength than the ones they had been accustomed to use. Hop dealers discouraged the use of California hops, because they thought it would interfere with their imported article. The brewers found after a while that it did not take near as many for a brewing, and they must not be boiled or steeped as long as the eastern hop. Now an eastern or foreign hop is a rarity in this market. It was early demonstrated that the soil and climate of Sacramento county was unsurpassed for hop culture. Here, and the only place known, a crop of from one to two thousand pounds per acre can be grown the first year the roots or sets are planted. It is a common occurrence to grow two and three thousand pounds per acre, and in some instances four thousand pounds have been grown on an acre.

"We have no frosts to affect them when in a dormant state in the winter, no vermin to effect them during growth, and no rains to destroy them during the gathering season.

"We use the willow, madrona and redwood hop poles, also the wire trellis for training. Most of the picking is done by Chinamen, a few Indians, and all the white help that will work. It is believed with our facilities and the great product per acre, that this coast can compete with the world in hop culture. The cost of picking green hops is from 80 cents to $1.00 per hundred pounds. Twenty-eight to thirty pounds of dry hops are obtained from 100 pounds of green. It is believed that hop culture will become one of the leading industries of this coast, and that she will gain the reputation and have the world for her market.

"In 1880 California grew 8,540 bales; in 1881, 8,913 bales; 1882, 14,227 bales; 1883, 27,000 bales; 1884, 41,231 bales; 1885, 26,183 bales; 1886, 28,411 bales. A bale of hops averages from 180 to 200 pounds."

Alfalfa.—This excellent forage plant is one of the "main stays" of the California farmer. Nothing would compensate him for the loss of this crop. It is valuable for pasturage, hay and seed. It is exceedingly vigorous, hardy and prolific; remains nearly dormant during November and December, and with this exception grows the year round. Three to five crops each year can be cut, ranging from two to four tons each cutting per acre. The last crop is usually taken for seed, for which a good market is found, the seed yielding from $30 to $40 per acre. All kinds of stock do well on it. Hogs fatten on it, and taken altogether its value is incalculable. The hay will sell at $6 to $10 per ton.

Beans.—Hundreds of car loads of beans are grown on the rich bottom lands of Sacramento county and each year are shipped to the eastern markets. They are a very profitable crop, and a failure has never been known.

Figs.—Most any part of California will produce this fruit. On the banks of the rivers in the county under consideration the fig tree attains to great size and is remarkably productive. The common black fig requires absolutely no care or attention. The tree grows like the oak, and is equally vigorous and hardy. It attains a great size, and when covered with its large green leaves and rich handsome fruit is a beautiful sight. The first crop is usually sold green, but the second is allowed to fall to the ground, and when sufficiently dry the figs are thrown into sacks and readily command three and one-half to five cents per pound, at which price they are very profitable.

The Smyrna, or "Fig of Commerce," is now being introduced, and there seems to be no good reason why California may not in the near future supply the millions of pounds of this delicious fruit that are annually consumed in the United States, and which are now imported from Europe.

Nuts.—Almonds have long been found a reliable and profitable crop. The tree will do well on any land that will grow peaches, and as the crop is rarely light and never fails the grower has a sure source of income from a fine almond orchard. At eleven to fourteen cents per pound, which is the ruling rate, they pay well.

Walnuts grow well here. The English soft shell walnut has not been extensively planted, but enough are growing to demonstrate that it is a profitable crop. Mr. P. H. Murphy has an English walnut tree on his ranch on the Cosumnes river, in Sacramento county, that is thought to be the largest in the state. This, however, may or may not be true, but it is a monstrous large tree and yields heavily of very fine quality. Black walnut trees are grown for shade and ornament. Peanuts of fine quality are extensively grown.

Broom corn is grown very extensively, as is also Egyptian corn; the latter making a good and cheap food for stock. Sweet potatoes do remarkably well, and are very largely cultivated by the Chinese, who also raise vast quantities of other kinds of vegetables. There is a grand opening for intelligent field gardening by skillful white growers. Cabbages, potatoes, onions, garlics, etc., etc., find a good market through the states and territories west of the Missouri river, and the growing of them cannot easily be overdone. Licorice is being successfully raised at Florin, in this county. The plant does well and may soon become a leading product.

No energetic man need fail to make a handsome profit, if, indeed, he does not secure a competency in growing any of the varied products herein mentioned. In horticulture he will, of course, need to use judgment and intelligence both in the selection of suitable land for the particular fruit desired and also in the varieties of fruit planted. It will be very desirable for him to consult some responsible nurseryman, of whom there are several in the county, as to the kinds of trees adapted to his land and as to the varieties most profitable. Finally the natural beauty and desirability of this section as a home will impress the thoughtful reader, when he considers the varied products, the mild and winterless climate, and the location of the county. A celebrated writer, Mr. Benj. F. Taylor, pays the following glowing tribute to Sacramento:

"The valley of the Sacramento is a garden, and Sacramento is the 'urbs in horto' of it. It is our first glimpse of the celestial flowery kingdom of the christian world. Roses never die. Rare exotics that we at the east cherish as if they were infants, and bend over like new made fathers and mothers, are distrained for conservatory rent and turned out of doors. The white dome of the state capitol rises like a pale planet above the green surges and waving banners of semi-tropic luxuriance * * *. The orange blossoms are abroad and the fruit is as golden as the three pawnbroker planets, and as green as a walnut in its first round about, all at once. They that dwell here sit under their own vine and fig tree, and the palm waves over their heads * * * * *. Taste and wealth have conspired with nature. There is no fairer landscape between the tropics."

FIRST FRUIT TRAIN FROM CALIFORNIA, LEAVING SACRAMENTO FOR THE EAST, 1886.

The same poetic writer also finds in Sacramento a fit theme for song when he writes the following describing his impressions of the valley on descending from the Sierras.

> "We die out of winter in the flash of an eye,
> Into Eden of earth, into heaven of sky;
> Sacramento's fair vale with its parlors of God,
> Where the souls of the flowers rise and drift all abroad,
> As if resurrection were all the year round
> And the writing of Christ sprang alive from the ground,
> When He said to the woman those words that will last
> When the globe shall grow human with the dead it has clasped.
> Live-oaks in their orchards, rare exotics run wild,
> No orphan among them, each Nature's own child.
> Oh, wonderful land where the turbulent sand
> Will burst into bloom at the touch of a hand,
> And a desert baptized prove an Eden disguised."

SOCIAL CONDITIONS IN SACRAMENTO.

By J. A. Woodson, Editor of the Sacramento Daily Record-Union.

"Who," asked George Eliot, "can all at once describe a human being?" How much less can one "all at once" describe the social condition of a community? A knowledge of society must be the result of viewing it in many phases; of long study and observation of it, and a judicial consideration of its strength and its weakness; of its springs and purposes, as distinguished from the dry leaves of formality. After more than thirty years' residence in California, from early to ripened manhood, and after nearly seventeen years of home life in California's capital city, the presumption should be in favor of fair judgment by a man of ordinary intelligence, whose active life has all related to social growth and development about him. So much for the witness who has noted social conditions in their transition from the nervous and restless pioneer era and the newness of a virgin country, to their "settling down" into the beaten paths of permanent industry.

Looking back, and then at the present, with as much of impartiality and mental equipoise as one ardently attached to the city of his home can command, I do not discover such marked difference between social conditions here, and those of the elder east, as many unacquainted with California are inclined to believe exists. It is foreign to the purpose of this paper to more than refer to the pioneer era, or that immediately preceding it. Out of the crude and variegated components of early society in California—a mingling of savagery and chivalry, of border rudeness and Mexican civilization, upon which the American began his work on these shores—have grown the present conditions.

False impressions concerning our society are entertained at the east, and they are due very largely to the romancing of a class of writers who have been accepted as true delineators of California life, when in fact they have drawn more largely upon exceptional events, rare characters, and their vivid fancy, than upon the fountains of truth. The California society of which Bret Harte, for instance, has written so much, is not a type of any existing representative conditions. The exaggerations of such writers—or, to state it more mildly, the exceptional characters and incidents upon which they have hinged their romantic romances—have grown, we fear, into accepted facts in the estimation of very many of our brethren abroad. The truth is, there is a logical relation between the early days of the era of gold discovery and the social conditions of this time, but it develops nothing to our discredit or which we should fear to have passed down into history.

In Sacramento, as in all the cities and towns of the state, property is as secure, life as carefully protected, education as much fostered, homes as sacred, woman as exalted, virtue as respected, probity as honored, as in the eldest and most staid of American communities. It is not true that in the primal days of our statehood there was that looseness of morals that has been charged and which it is by some believed is still reflected in the moral tone of the present. The pioneer men of California were picked and chosen; they were adventurous spirits, but came out of the best civilization of the great east. They were representative of the homes of the whole Union, chivalrous, daring, moved by the same impulses and actuated by the same motives as their brethren at home. Such as remained in the land and grew into the new conditions inseparable from settlement of the country, tilling of the soil and the influx of commercial conservatism, have proved to the world their capacity as state builders, and that the social foundations they laid were not ill planted. They have lived to see the work of their hands develop a code of laws modeled after the best accepted systems; to witness the uprise of a school system so richly endowed as to excite the admiration of the world, and afford the youth of the state almost boundless opportunities for intellectual culture and mental training. Whatever high-minded and courageous pioneers, commercial activity, legitimate industries, agricultural development, financial ability, and the bounty of nature in her fairest part and most generous mood, could do for any people, they have done for California, and essentially for Sacramento. With the moral influence of the church and the school these factors have given us society where lawlessness is no more known than in cities of like population and similar surroundings at the east. The aspirations of the people of the great valley, of which Sacramento is the commercial seat, are as high, and their purposes as pure as those of any other people. We resist the evil tendencies of human nature with quite as much vigor as any; we are as sensitive to debasing influences and as solicitous for their elimination from society, as are our eastern friends.

These are generalities, and yet no more definite idea can be conveyed to the stranger of social conditions in Sacramento, except by a detailed statement of the forms social activities have taken. To this end I may recite that the school system of the state, unprecedented in endowment, is supplemented in our city by self-imposition of a still greater tax to bring the scheme of education to a still higher standard. Nowhere in the state is greater interest manifested in education of the youth, and nowhere are the common schools and high schools better equipped and turning out better results. The church is maintained in all its branches, and all the church organizations are maintained with a liberal hand. All the customary confraternal associations are represented in our city, and nowhere else is their membership of a higher order of citizenship. Libraries are plentiful and are patronized to a gratifying extent. The city owns a superb art gallery, and appreciation of the rare works within it is manifest by the constant visitations paid to it by the masses. An art school is maintained by a popular and scientific association. Asylums and hospitals, benevolent associations and charitable organizations commensurate with our needs, are supported by the generosity of the people. Literary circles, clubs and associations, in large number, testify to the intellectual tastes of the people. Social societies to cater to the natural desire for rational amusement are formed from time to time, and have varying terms

E. B. CROCKER ART GALLERY, SACRAMENTO.

of life. The demand for newspapers and periodicals is responded to by five journals and a magazine, and several papers of irregular issue. The dramatic taste is favored by the appearance of companies in two handsome theatres, and the audiences are uniformly critical and just; so much so as to make their judgment feared by the unworthy and courted by the meritorious.

There is ample wealth in Sacramento, but practically none of the arrogance that is so frequently its accompaniment; indeed, no community in the country is so free from offensive manifestations of purse pride—a fact upon which I am disposed to place great emphasis. The homes of the city constitute the chief source of the pride of its people—a truth which more than any other will give the intelligent reader a correct idea of our social conditions. I have, in seventeen years' residence among them, found the people who really constitute the community broad-minded, generous, susceptible to all humanizing, refining and gentle influences, and abhorrent of the coarse, narrow, illiberal and vicious. On the other hand, that no concealments may be made, it is true that there is lack of that spirit of providence characteristic of our eastern brethren. The contention with nature here for subsistence is so slight that men place a lower estimate upon the need for saving, and gratify their tastes with more liberality of expenditure and less care for the morrow. The restraints that in older communities secure a greater regard for the Christian Sabbath are somewhat less felt here, as throughout all California. The city is not free from other ills that afflict all large aggregations of population, but nowhere is the vicious criminal element kept under stronger check or does it feel more of repressive vigor. Gaming, save on rare occasions, when there is an outburst of audacity, is driven to hole and corner, and probably is not practiced more extensively than in many metropolitan communities at the east.

To sum up: With precisely the evils which intelligence will suggest as likely to exist in a city situated upon several great arteries of transportation and communication, Sacramento's social and refining influences, her intellectual and moral forces, the potency of her home influence, the leveling of moneyed distinctions and the association of the people upon the basis of worth, intelligence and moral character; the remarkable minimum of the criminal and vicious elements; the strong manifestations of fine taste for art, music and literature; the conservative influences of an immense and immediately occupied agricultural area; the large proportion of the best representatives of the older states, who have taken up their residence here; the character and condition and numerical strength of the churches; the breadth and height of the educational institutions of the city, public and private; the metropolitan privilege and the rural conservatism which characterize Sacramento—all these convince me that the social conditions in this city invite the commendation of the stranger and challenge his criticism.

CLIMATE AND RAINFALL.

By Sergeant James A. Barwick, Observer Signal Corps, U. S. Army and Meteorologist to the California State Board of Agriculture.

The climatic condition of Sacramento county as compared with the same condition of the great Riviera and citrus and olive belt of northern and western Italy, and also between our county and North Carolina, we find that this county leads both Italy and North Carolina. Table 2 shows the average winter, spring, summer, autumn and yearly temperature, along with the highest and lowest temperatures and average rainfall of Sacramento, Brighton and Galt. The mean of these three points gives us the average temperature of Sacramento county as compared with the seven points in northern Italy, (see Table 2), which is very little larger than our county. It is found that Sacramento county shows a warmer winter, spring and yearly average temperature and about the same summer and autumn temperature that the great citrus belt of northern Italy does, where it is said "perpetual summer exists, skies are blue and the sun ever shines." The comparative records show that this is an unwarranted liberty taken by the writers of the climate of northern Italy. Compare the climate of Sacramento county with the Italian, (see Table 4), and ours is found to excel theirs in winter and spring, equal them in summer and autumn, and excel them in the mean average temperature for the year. Their average number of clear days in a year numbers 224, while Sacramento county has an average of 240, being more clear days in a year than any inhabited portion of the northern hemisphere, except Yuma, Arizona, which has 279; but the climate of

RESOURCES OF SACRAMENTO COUNTY. 43

Table 1.

Weather Review for—	1878.	1879.	1880.	1881.	1882.	1883.	1884.	1885.	1886.
Average temperature	61.3	60.3	57.2	59.2	58.5	58.8	58.8	61.2	58.8
Highest temperature	100.5	103.0	98.0	98.6	99.8	103.5	100.0	105.0	105.0
Lowest temperature	23.5	25.0	25.0	31.9	27.0	22.0	21.0	34.2	27.5
Range of temperature	77.0	78.0	73.0	66.7	72.8	81.5	79.0	70.8	77.5
Greatest monthly range of temperature	50.0	49.0	49.0	46.7	55.2	55.8	46.0	58.0	52.8
Least monthly range of temperature	21.0	33.7	25.0	27.0	31.6	35.7	30.0	27.0	33.2
Average maximum temperature	81.5	83.7	80.0	81.6	82.0	84.3	80.3	85.2	83.9
Average minimum temperature	41.2	41.2	39.9	42.1	40.1	39.8	41.5	45.3	41.3
Average range of temperature	40.3	42.5	40.1	39.5	41.9	44.5	38.8	39.9	42.6
Average humidity	62.2	65.7	64.6	66.7	66.0	69.0	70.7	67.8	70.1
Average dew point					45.7	47.3	48.5	48.8	47.8
Prevailing direction of wind	S.	S.	S.	S.	S.	S.	S.	S.	S.E.
Total rainfall	23.45	22.37	31.99	20.71	18.06	13.48	34.92	20.72	18.17
Total velocity wind	52.830	52.214	62.497	57.846	58.674	52.637	62.611	62.405	56.036
Maximum velocity wind	40	39	40	32	35	36	36	36	44
Direction at the time of maximum velocity	N.	S.	S.E.	S.E.	N.	N.W.	N.W.	S.E.	S.E.
Total number of clear days	234	208	237	251	249	263	239	227	262
Total number of fair days	75	99	59	69	76	76	68	88	76
Total number of cloudy days	56	58	70	45	40	26	59	50	37
Total number of foggy days	0	4	5	8	1	11	0	0	4
Total number of days rain fell	66	79	70	67	70	54	76	62	57
Total number of earthquakes	2	0	0	1	0	0	0	2	1
Snow storms	0	1	1	0	3	2	0	0	0
Thunder and lightning	4	4	3	4	4	2	3	6	3
Light frosts	18	17	14	34	69	33	31	24	30
Heavy frosts	22	27	32	4	12	40	22	0	10
Total number days max. temperature above 90°	35	48	16	18	43	45	22	49	45
Total number days min. temperature below 32°	15	14	17	1	5	27	13	0	4

Yuma is incomparable with ours—we excel it in salubrity and healthfulness.

The tables will be found interesting as well as instructive.

Table 1 gives a general comparison of the weather in all its features (at Sacramento city), as taken from the records of the United States signal office and shows the comparisons of the same from 1878 to 1886 inclusive—a period of nine years. These conditions will hold good for the entire county, it being somewhat warmer in the vicinity of Galt, in the southern portion. This table gives the average yearly, and highest and lowest temperatures; average maximum and minimum temperatures; average humidity or relative amount of moisture in the atmosphere; average dew point; prevailing direction of wind; total rainfall; total velocity of wind and the maximum hourly velocity; number of clear, fair and cloudy days and days rain fell; number of light and heavy frosts and number of days maximum temperature was above 90° and below 32°, etc.

Table 2.

This table gives the average temperature for each season of the year, along with the highest and lowest temperature and average rainfall for Sacramento, Brighton and Galt. The mean of these three places gives the average mean for this county.

Places in Sacramento County.	Average winter temperature.	Average spring temperature.	Aver'e summer temperature.	Aver'e autumn temperature.	Average yearly (or annual) temperat're	Highest temperature.	Lowest temperature.	Average rainfall (in inches).
Sacramento	48.3	59.5	71.7	61.5	60.2	106	19.94	19
Brighton	47.4	59.9	74.8	61.9	61.2	109	16.44	20
Galt	48.5	61.7	76.4	62.6	62.3	108	15.70	19
Average temp. and rainfall of the county	48.1	60.4	74.3	62.0	61.2	100*	17.36	19 *

*Highest and lowest temperature.

Note.—The elevation above sea level is as follows: Sacramento 30 feet; Brighton 53 feet, and Galt 49 feet. The latitude and longitude of Sacramento city is north latitude 38 degrees and 35 minutes. Longitude west from Greenwich 121 degrees and 30 minutes.

Table 3.

The following tabulated data gives the average temperature for the year and for each season; along with the highest and lowest temperature and clear days for several places. The average for all the places named in the table give the average mean for northern Italy, where oranges, lemons and olives flourish.

PLACES IN THE CITRUS AND OLIVE BELT OF NORTHERN ITALY.	Average winter temperature	Average spring temperature	Aver'e summer temperature	Aver'e autumn temperature	Average yearly temperature	Highest temperature	Lowest temperature	Average
Florence	44.3	56.0	74.0	60.7	58.8			
Pisa	46.4	57.2	75.2	62.8	60.4			
Genoa	44.9	58.6	75.0	63.0	60.4			
San Remo	48.9	57.3	72.4	61.9	60.1	85	25	
Mentone	49.0	58.3	73.9	62.5	60.9	85	23	214
Nice	47.8	56.2	72.3	61.6	59.5			229
Cannes	49.6	57.4	73.1	61.0	60.2	85	20	
Mean tem. North. Italy	47.3	57.3	73.7	61.9	60.0	85.0	22.7	221

Table 4.

This table shows briefly the figures of comparison between Sacramento county, northern Italy and North Carolina, giving the average temperature by seasons and for the year, with the highest and lowest temperature and average number of clear days.

NAMES OF PLACES.	Average winter temperature	Average spring temperature	Aver'e summer temperature	Aver'e autumn temperature	Average yearly temperature	Highest temperature	Lowest temperature	Average number of clear days
Sacramento County	48.1	60.4	74.3	62.0	61.2	109	19	240
Northern Italy	47.4	57.3	73.7	61.9	60.0	85	20	221
North Carolina	46.3	59.5	77.6	64.0	61.9	103	*5	116

* Below zero.

PRIMARY SCHOOL BUILDING, SACRAMENTO CITY.

THERE yet remains in this State many thousand acres of available lands subject to entry under the United States and State laws. These lands are situated either in the foothills of the Sierra Nevada and Coast Ranges of mountains, or on the broad plains of the San Joaquin and Sacramento Valleys. They are lands which in the rush and excitement of earlier periods, when settlers could make their selection from almost the entire State, were either overlooked or regarded as of small importance. Recent history of California conclusively shows that some of the most profitable lands we have are those which were a few years ago considered worthless. Improved systems of irrigation and scientific modes of cultivation have accomplished this change of sentiment. The old fossilized ideas of farming are fast making room for improved and more practical methods, and, as a consequence, the "waste" lands of Californa exist only as a Pioneer reminiscence.

On the yet unsettled great plains of this State, where the rainfall is often inadequate to meet the demand, artesian wells have made it possible for the settler to cease dependence on the elements, and has enabled him to declare his independence of the laws governing riparian ownership of water; thus lands heretofore surrendered to stockmen for grazing purposes are fast becoming recognized for their real worth. The mining camps of the foothills, which have remained dormant and deserted since the golden days of '49, are now teeming with a new activity and bustle, as permanent as it is profitable, and to-day the "dumps," "tailings," "gulches," and "cañons" are producing more "color" than they ever yielded in the palmy days of yore.

For years I have devoted my entire attention to this question, and to a study of the laws governing the location of public lands; and the results have clearly proven that the labor was not in vain. Although California is the second State in the Union, as regards size, there is very little of her territory I have not personally and carefully inspected; and there is no township within her vast borders, where vacant lands exist, from which I cannot furnish an abstract of title.

Under the laws of this State an applicant is entitled to locate any portion of one section, or 640 acres of school land, without residence thereon, at the minimum price of $1.25 per acre. Of this sum 20 per cent of the purchase money (or 25 cents per acre) must be paid ninety days after entry, with interest on deferred payment at the rate of 7 per cent per annum until paid—it being optional with the purchaser to pay in full or permit the balance of $1.00 per acre to remain at interest.

My charges for adjusting land claims are moderate compared to the high prices asked for lands of no better quality; and as an investment there is nothing so safe or sure under the sun. To those desirous of securing good cheap lands anywhere in the State, I can truthfully say that my facilities for giving satisfaction far exceed all other dealers combined, as an enormous number of patrons in various portions of the State can readily testify.

Correspondents residing at a distance must accompany each letter of inquiry with a sum not less than $5.00 to insure attention and as an evidence of good faith. In the event of further business transactions, this sum will be deducted from the final amount to be paid.

Call on or address

HORACE STEVENS.

Attorney for Land Claimants,

No. 1525 N Street,

Sacramento, California.

SACRAMENTO AS A NATURAL TRADE CENTER.

By C. K. McClatchy, Managing Editor Sacramento Daily Evening Bee.

Sacramento, situated as she is, the center and metropolis of the richest portion of California, the very heart of a vast railroad system, and with magnificent water power right at her very doors, presents advantages to intending investors in manufactures equalled by no city on the Pacific slope. That this is so is amply proved by the presence here of the vast shops of the Southern Pacific Company, in which they build their own cars, locomotives, and general rolling stock, and do their own repairing. Notwithstanding they are offered all the land free near Rocklin they could use, and right on the line of the railroad, the shrewd directors—with an eye to the advantages of the present and the wonderful probabilities of the future—wisely decided to obtain land in this city, where every conceivable convenience would be right at their very hands. The result has been that to-day their buildings occupy some thirty acres; that there are employed therein over 2,000 men, with a pay-roll of $120,000 per month. This alone should be sufficient to demonstrate the inducements which Sacramento offers as aids to manufacture. These shops are situated within a stone's throw of the Sacramento river, and within easy reach of the American on the north. Here is a magnificent water power rushing past their open doors every day in the year, and the company intend to take advantage of it in several of their shops as soon as they can make the necessary arrangements.

But while the railroad shops are the prominent manufacturing interests of Sacramento, they are by no means the only one, and the others should not be lost sight of. For instance, there are three great and extensive flouring mills right in our midst. These mills send broadcast all over the world some 60,000,000 pounds of flour annually, or about 300,000 barrels. The millers in Sacramento have several advantages of location. In the first place, owing to the fact of a lesser tariff for freight; wheat can always be brought here at $1.00 a ton less than the ruling rates at San Francisco. It takes about a ton and a half of wheat to make a ton of flour, and so it follows that flour can be manufactured here about 15 cents a barrel cheaper than in San Francisco. That, then, gives millers here an even chance on ocean shipments, while they have immeasurably the best of it on all inland consignments. Besides, these mills are right on the direct line of railroad and river travel.

Sacramento also has three iron foundries, which turn out large quantities of most superior work. She possessed a woolen mill, which became noted for the excellence of its goods all over the coast, but which was unfortunately burned down. For many years a beet sugar factory was in operation, and its buildings stand to-day reproachful monuments to mismanagement. There is no reason why a beet sugar factory should not pay well here if properly conducted, in the hands of a skillful and skilled foreman. Every imaginable advantage can here be found. Sacramento also possessed an extensive smelting works, but that, too, was in the hands of men new to the management of such an establishment, and fire subsequently finished the disasters which incompetency had inaugurated.

The manufacture of brick is a very extensive industry in Sacramento county. The supply of the best soil to be found anywhere for this purpose is inexhaustible, and Sacramento county brick has a name all over the coast. Here, again, transportation facilities, both by land and water, are unsurpassed. There are half a dozen breweries in Sacramento city which do a thriving business. As Sacramento is one of the great hop countries of the world, the brewers have their materials at their very doors.

Scores of other manufactories might be enumerated—carriage, buggy and wagon manufactories, furniture manufactories, manufactories of sashes, doors and blinds, extensive sawmills, potteries, box factories, soap factories, and many others. But the space to be devoted to this article is limited, and the purpose thereof is not so much to show what we now have, as to concisely present to the outside world all the manifold advantages which Sacramento offers for the establishment of profitable manufactories of all kinds.

The object, then, being to place the manifold advantages of Sacramento as a manufacturing center prominently before the eyes of intending immigrants and expectant capitalists, it is not so much desirable to present before them what we have already in the line of manufactories, as to show them the reasons why Sacramento offers them inducements for the establishment of such manufactories that cannot be rivalled anywhere. Some of these inducements might be enumerated thus:

Availability.—Sacramento is the center almost of the state. It is ironed by railroads and lapped by rivers. Twenty-seven trains dart past it every day. It is the pivot of traffic, the magnet of travel. Freight from the four centers has to pass through this capital city of the golden state, and the vast bulk of overland travel skirts by her doors. Through her extensive system of railroad and river communication, this city taps all of Northern and Central California. The city, then, is thoroughly known all over this section of the state, and knowledge makes the market.

Salubrity.—Statistics prove that Sacramento is the second healthiest city in the United States; Auburn, New York, being given the first place. When men desire to locate anywhere, either for business or for pleasure, the above of itself is a sterling recommendation.

Motive Power.—It would be possible to enumerate a dozen other advantages possessed by this city as a site for manufactories, but space forbids. The one great and overshadowing merit she has in this matter is the wonderful water power right at her very gates, which can be had and utilized for a song. The limpid Sacramento comes caressingly down past the very breast, while the impetuous American dashes over her shoulders. There is latent power enough in the latter river to run all the manufactories of Massachusetts. Figures have proven that there is frequently a fall of 20 feet in that river at Folsom in 24 hours. What a tremendous power that is, if properly applied! Why, it could make the banks of the American and the Sacramento rivers echo to the sound of hammer and forge, of tongs and anvils, while the music of the bellows whistled to the rushing stream. There are really no such advantages for manufactories presented on the Pacific slope as are offered in Sacramento.

SACRAMENTO AND ADJACENT COUNTIES.

By Geo. W. Hancock, Director of the State Agricultural Society.

Sacramento county is the most peculiar in its character of the counties of California. Formerly it was a fine stock county, with herds of cattle and bands of horses roaming at will over its plains and rich bottom lands. But when these large stock interests retired before the varied branches of agriculture—general farming, fruit growing and market gardening—Sacramento county was tried in a furnace of fire. It never has proved to be a successful section for the production of cereals when compared with the counties of Sutter, Butte, Tehama, Colusa and Yolo. While it is true that none of the counties named have so much first-class bottom land, it is also a fact that they have an even grade or average of land that returns a good profit to all who till the soil within their bounds.

While it is also true that no other section of the state is so well supplied with water readily available for purposes of irrigation, yet it has been allowed to run idly to the sea, except in a few instances of individual effort. There is no other locality in the state where the soil will respond so bountifully when irrigated as the upland districts of Sacramento county, and there is no other section where one system of irrigation will cover so much territory with an abundant supply at so small a cost. The American and Cosumnes rivers traverse the county from the hills on the northeast to the Sacramento river on the southwest, carrying a volume of water that will, if used upon the land, treble the product of every acre in the upland section of the county. On the Sacramento river the land is so rich and moist that irrigation has never been a necessity. Twice in the American history of California it might have been applied to advantage, by placing pumps on the river bank and raising the water from that inexhaustible stream. By that simple means every farm could be irrigated at a cost that, when considered in a fruit crop, would not be appreciable in the expense account.

Hops have been a remarkably remunerative crop in Sacramento county. The hop lands border on the American, Cosumnes and Sacramento rivers. A. Menke, on the American river, boasts of the largest hop-yard in the world—the annual yield of which often reaches 3,000 pounds per acre, and $80,000 worth have been produced from 50 acres in one crop.

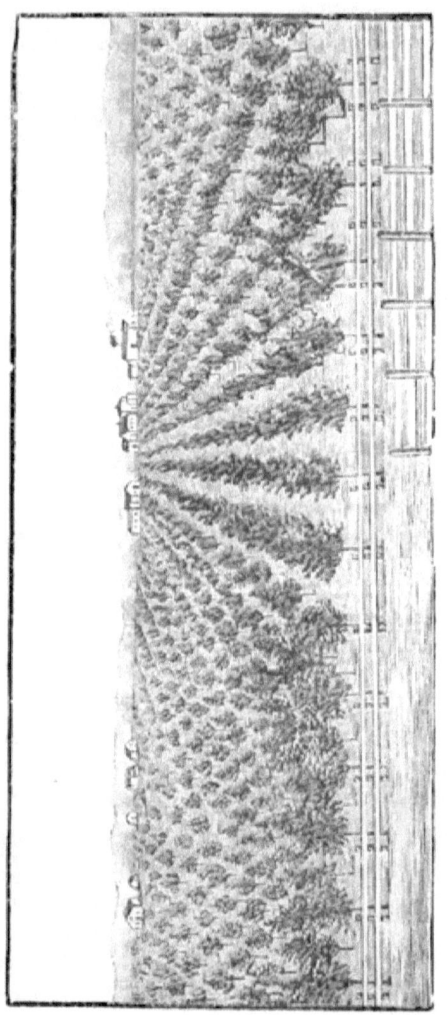

REED AND VAN GUELDER ORCHARD, SACRAMENTO.

Alfalfa is another crop that is exceptionally profitable as a forage crop on the bottom or irrigated lands, often producing 10 to 15 tons of cured hay per acre. In using the crop for pasturage it has kept 15 to 18 head of sheep to the acre for eight months of the growing season, and has been known to keep more than one horse per acre where several hundred run in a band the whole year round.

Sacramento is essentially a fruit county of the most varied capacity. Strawberries, raspberries, blackberries, cherries, apricots, plums, prunes, peaches, pears, apples, raisin and table grapes, nuts of every variety, figs, oranges, lemons, limes and pomegranates all grow and produce in luxuriance and abundance. Other localities may fairly rival us in the production of some of these fruits, but we produce them all in the utmost perfection, and every acre of land in Sacramento county—except the swamp and overflowed area—is first-class fruit land, with or without irrigation.

There is here and there a thermal belt or a fruit section, but it is one grand whole, every 20 acres being capable of supporting a family in competence if judiciously planted and thoroughly and properly cultivated. Planted in the fruits above named, the lands of Sacramento county, in the past and present, have returned and will return $200, $500, $1,000, $1,500 and more per acre per annum. It has been practically demonstrated that one acre of Bartlett pears near Sacramento city brought $1,500 for one crop, $800 for the next, and $600 for the next, yet the land had not been cultivated or the trees pruned in that time. It is also known that a young orchard of 18 acres of Bartlett pears yielded $500 per acre net per annum. The yield of the Natoma vineyard of table grapes in 1886 returned, exclusive of freight and commissions, $270 per acre.

Sacramento county has 200,000 acres of land practically vacant, which can be had from $25 to $100 per acre, and which when planted to trees and vines and in bearing will yield an income on an investment of from $500 to $2,000 per acre per annum. Many choice improved places in this county cannot now be had for $1,000 per acre. The production of fruit is becoming more and more a fine art. The condition in which it will reach an eastern market is an important consideration in its value. There it must be fair to look at, rich in sugar, and firm in its resistance to decay. Such fruit is produced in Sacramento county in greater uniformity and over a larger proportional area than in any other county. El Dorado, Placer and Yuba have their foothill thermal belts, by no means meager or insignificant in extent and importance, and they are strong and consistent rivals of Sacramento as to attractiveness to the eye and shipping quality of their fruit. The plains section of Placer, Yuba and Sutter will in the future develop into a rich raisin and table grape district.

To Placer county has been already awarded the credit of producing a raisin equal if not superior to the five crown De Hiser raisin of France, which until equaled here had no rival in quality in the world. The product of one acre irrigated of these raisins has been as high as $600 per annum.

Sutter county being entirely a valley county, except the lone Buttes in its northern bounds, has also fine fruit and grape lands, the choicest fruit lands lying on the banks of the Feather and Sacramento rivers. Sutter has spots of as fine fruit land as the State can boast of.

To the north of Sutter lies Butte county, one half mountain and one half valley. Its valley lands are among the best for general farming of any in the State. Butte can boast of the largest area of land covered with majestic oak timber of any valley county, and this timber belt will in the near future develop the very best fruit land. The fine orchard of General Bidwell and the extensive vineyard farms of Governor Standford are within its bounds. They speak more than volumes of the productiveness of the Butte county fruit and grape lands.

To the north of Butte lies the county of Tehama, having within her confines the head of the Sacramento valley. The lands on the east side of the Sacramento river stretch to the foothills, and are a close imitation of the oak park land of Butte county, but more even in their quality and better adapted to fruit culture. Returning south we will cross the river and there we find a more varied quality of land, much of it needing irrigation to make fruit production most profitable. Tehama county is cut on both sides of the Sacramento river by small streams that flow from her hills to the great drain of the valley, and its lands are therefore susceptible of irrigation.

South of Tehama, on the west bank of the Sacramento river, lies Colusa county, the banner wheat county of the world. There very little attention has been paid to fruit raising as a source of income, yet there are large portions of it that will be planted to orchards and vineyards at no distant day. The yield of wheat in Colusa county furnishes undeniable proof that its soil will liberally respond when planted to vines and trees.

South of Colusa lies Yolo. There is nothing that can speak in more affirmative language of its prosperity than the fact that Woodland, its county seat, is the wealthiest town of its size in the world. Yolo has some of the best raisin vineyards in the State and also some of the choicest orchard lands.

All these sections are tributary to the business of Sacramento city, and that city will grow and prosper with their growth and prosperity.

There is no portion in California where land is so cheap, measured by its productive capacity, as in Sacramento county. There is no place where the excessive heat of the summer is covered by so few days as at Sacramento city. No other place has so many sunny days in a year. No other place in the warm sections of California is so nicely tempered with moisture, which cools the atmosphere without making it either chilly or muggy. There is no other place, where spring and autumn reach so far into the seasons of summer and winter. Northern California is the natural orchard and vineyard section of the world. The home seeker has but to be judicious in his selection of locality and purchase, and then let him plant understandingly, and he is sure to gather an appropriate reward for his toil.

A FACT

WE WANT TO IMPRESS upon the minds of all people east of the Rocky Mountains is, *That for Fruit-growing Sacramento Valley is the Garden Spot of California.* There is an impression abroad—owing to excellent advertising of that section—that Southern California comprises all that is good of the whole State. The facts are, that for the year 1886 the shipments of fruit—outside of oranges—were less than 300,000 pounds for the whole of Southern California, while Sacramento City *alone* shipped, besides oranges, 18,954,000 pounds of green fruits—and the figures for 1887 bid fair to double those for 1886. These are solid facts for the southern boomers to digest at their leisure.

Having impressed that fact on your mind, we now want to call your attention to two more facts, namely: Land in the Sacramento valley, that will produce anything in the shape of fruit, can be had from one-quarter to one-tenth the price of similar land in Southern California. The other fact is: The headquarters for farms, large and small, is the office of

A. LEONARD & SON,
REAL ESTATE AGENTS,
No. 1014 Fourth Street,
Sacramento, California.

WEIL & JOHNSON,
Real Estate Agents
SACRAMENTO, CALIFORNIA,

Respectfully call the attention of all parties seeking homes and investments in California to a few of the many reasons why Sacramento City and vicinity is the most desirable place in which to locate.

First—It is most eligibly situated, in the center of the largest and most fertile valley (the great Sacramento) in the State of California.

Second—Because San Francisco alone leads it as a business center.

Third—Because its climate is unsurpassed, and the productiveness of its soil unequaled.

Fourth—Because ninety per cent of all the fruit is grown adjacent to and shipped from Sacramento, the Capital of the State.

Fifth—Because its schools and educational advantages are among the best.

We have on our list lands of all descriptions, suitable for grain, fruit and vine culture, at prices within the reach of all.

Reliable information cheerfully given. Correspondence solicited.

FOR **Homes amid Fruits and Flowers,** CALL ON
WEIL & JOHNSON, REAL ESTATE AGENTS
402 J Street, Sacramento, California.

THE PRODUCE SHIPPED FROM SACRAMENTO.

By Eugene J. Gregory, Mayor of the City of Sacramento.

Sacramento, by reason of her natural resources, geographical relation to the various producing sections, and admirable transportation facilities, deservedly sustains the reputation of being the largest fruit and vegetable shipping point in the state, and is the recognized outlet for the products of Central and Northern California. These facts are fully established by statistics, which demonstrate that the industries mentioned have constantly strengthened and increased until both are now powerful factors in the prosperity of California. From the commencement the increase has been extraordinary. When the hardy pioneer allotted an occasional hour from his search for gold to till the soil and plant a few trees—for either benefit or decoration of his then primitive surroundings—he little thought that he was unconsciously sowing the seeds of a great industry which was destined to reach such vast proportions as to ultimately overshadow all other pursuits and enterprises—that he was paving the way for commercial prosperity in our state; such is now the case, especially in Sacramento county, in the possession of manifold natural advantages in climate, soil and productions. Within its borders every kind, character and variety of agricultural, horticultural and viticultural products thrive, and in abundance, the excellence of which command universal and almost unlimited demand from all portions of the civilized world.

Although the crop of 1887 was the largest known in the history of our state, yet the requirements have been greater than the supply—a condition which clearly proves that the industry is still in its infancy, and that the production and output must necessarily increase, until its magnitude will be something enormous to contemplate.

The carload shipments from Sacramento during 1887 amounted to the enormous figures of 32,604,000 pounds of green fruit and vegetables—an increase of over 85 per cent. against the season of 1886, while that particular year had gained in the some proportion over its predecessor. These shipments were distributed in every quarter of the United States, Canada and Mexico, as well as in the islands of the Pacific Ocean, while a very large quantity has been successfully transported to various European markets—London, Paris, Edinburgh, Glasgow, Galway, etc. When ocean transportation methods are improved and facilitated we may confidently look forward to a large and extensive export outlet for our products.

Our dried and canned products readily command the world for a market—an advantage that is possessed by California alone, regardless of product or staple. This particular and important branch of the industry has already assumed standard record and does not, therefore, require comment at my hands.

In the vegetable product our resources show a never-failing yield of choice quality and desirable variety, which—from the generous influences of climate, soil and season is Sacramento county so greatly blessed—places that staple before us in such abundance and excellence as to be looked upon by our people as a useful and necessary commodity, while to our friends in all other portions of the Union it is regarded in the light of a luxury, and as such, are transported by the carload to every city of importance in the United States. The articles of potatoes, cabbage, onions, etc., are sent to Chicago, New York, Philadelphia, St. Louis, Kansas City, Omaha, Denver, New Orleans, Galveston, etc., in carload lots, which at the end of the season count up into the hundreds.

These facts readily demonstrate the claims of Sacramento city and county for excellence of climate, magnificence of products and facilities—and the progressive spirit which animates her people in the earnest desire to promote and strengthen our interests, resources and advantages. With the immense acreage of fruit and vegetables now in bearing, and the acquisition of numberless new orchards, vineyards and farms, it is a safe prediction that within a few years these industries will finally supersede all other pursuits wherein the question of soil and climate are concerned, and practically and forcibly perpetuate the reputation that California now enjoys—as being the "garden state of the world."

THOROUGHBRED HORSES.

By JOHN A. SHEEHAN, of the Sacramento Daily Bee.

No state in the Union has more complete and valuable advantages for the stock grown than California, and it cannot be long, if present indications mean anything, when she will take precedence even of the far-famed Kentucky in the number and extent of her foaling farms. Indeed, it has come to pass that no race in the broad east, from New Orleans to New York, is considered worth material attention unless it have one or more representative from the great stock farms of the golden state.

It is of peculiar pride with the people of Sacramento county to remember that the most famous stables of the state are within her borders. It is a fact that the largest stock farm devoted to horses in America is located in Sacramento county, and only a few miles from the capital city. Reference is particularly made to the great breeding farm of J. B. Haggin, to the north of the city of Sacramento. Here the thoroughbred running and the trotting horses are brought to their highest degree of perfection, and all over the nation their fame has gone. The land of the Bourbon can not in its highest glory boast of so far-famed and extensive a breeding-farm as this. The five most noted of California stock farms are Rancho del Paso, Santa Anita, Palo Alto, Arno and Rancho del Rio, and it may be said, with a bold challenge to all disputers, that these are not to be excelled by the best in England or America. And why should this not be true? Here is the superbest of climates. Here can be grown the choicest of feed. Here there is every incentive in the realm of nature for the production of the highest types of the breeder's skill. The days are rare or never come when the finset horses may not be exercised, and the climate is likewise decidedly in favor of the fast possibilities of the young and growing animal.

The Rancho del Paso, five miles north of Sacramento, contains 44,000 acres. John Mackay is the superintendent, and it is since he assumed its management that Rancho del Paso began to take the foremost position it now occupies. The trotters and thoroughbreds are kept in different parts of the farm, and good exercising tracks are maintained for both. Considerable of the more recent fame of the farm depends upon the Irish stallion Kyrle Daly, by Artillery, dam Colleen Rhue, by Gemma-di-Vergy. Next to imp. Kyrle Daly was Longfield by Monarchist, Wheatby by War Dance, and Jim Brown by Foster.

The horses that have been heard from in the east from Rancho del Paso are too well known to need mentioning, and it is enough to know that they have gallantly maintained the claims of Sacramento county as the bright particular spot in California for the development of the finest thoroughbred horses. The famous Hambletonian stud, Echo, at the head of the trotting stock, is known through his fleet and robust progeny throughout the State. Besides Echo are the stallions Norwood, Alaska and Algona. Although it cannot be said that Mr. Haggin has made any special effort to breed fancy trotters, it must be said that colts from his farm have become very popular as substantial roadsters with the people of California. The annual sale of horses from the Rancho Del Paso have come to be considered great opportunities for lovers of the horse, and one sale of 130 head, at an average price of $400 each, satisfactorily demonstrates this.

Everybody in the Sacramento valley knows the splendid Rancho del Rio, four miles south of the capital city. No site could be more delightful. The stables, track and residences are situated on a knoll, rising several feet above the ground around. It was the proprietor of the Rancho del Rio, Mr. Winters, who bought the unconquerable Norfolk for $15,000, and thus laid the foundation for a stable which has since become famous. Mr. Winters has conformed himself to the breeding of thoroughbreds exclusively, and in this respect ranks with the oldest breeders in America. The son of the great Lexington has no superior among the famous sires of the day. Joe Hooker was another of Winters' famous stallions whose get have given him a great name.

Then we have in this county the Arno stud farm, 20 miles southeast of Sacramento city. W. L. Pritchard also has done a great deal to establish the name of Sacramento as a favored section for the breeding of fine horses, and we have said nothing of Dr. M. W. Hicks and others who have bred some of the best horses that ever stepped in California. Enough has been shown to establish the main fact—that nowhere in the country can the stock-breeder find more nearly perfect conditions for his business than right here.

In Sacramento city is the fastest and best track in the state and a great favorite with horsemen ambitious to make a record for their stud.

ST. GEORGE BUILDING, SACRAMENTO.

The St. George Building, an engraving of which appears above, is one of the most imposing structures in the city. It is situated on the southeast corner of J and Fourth streets, and is owned by the Odd Fellows' Hall Association, incorporated in 1866, and occupied by the People's Savings Bank, several leading real estate and insurance offices, and numerous other classes of business. Directors: F. W. Fratt, Wm. Beckman, Robt. Devlin, W. C. Felch, and Geo. F. Parker. W. C. Felch, President. Geo. F. Parker, Secretary.

EDUCATIONAL.

By ELWOOD BRUNER, District Attorney of Sacramento County.

One of the most important advantages which the resident of Sacramento county possesses, is the opportunity to educate his children either in the public or private schools. Early in its history those having charge of the public schools, with wise foresight, provided liberally for their sustenance, and as a result, throughout both city and county, the buildings are large and commodious, the libraries stocked with choice literature, and the mechanical apparatus sufficient and in good repair. No debts have accrued on school property, and the tax-payers are able and willing to provide liberally for the increased wants of a people rapidly growing in wealth and numbers.

It will be impossible in the brief limits of this article to more than outline the character and extent of the educational facilities of Sacramento city and county.

The public schools of Sacramento city are thirteen in number, and are classified as follows: One high school, with five teachers; two grammar schools, with twenty-six teachers; nine primary schools, with thirty-six teachers; and one night school, with two teachers. In addition to the above there are four teachers of ungraded classes and four substitute teachers, making a total of seventy-seven teachers under the supervision of the Board of Education of Sacramento city.

The total number of census children in Sacramento city between five and seventeen years of age, is six thousand and sixty-seven, of whom three thousand two hundred and fifty-seven are enrolled in the public schools, and about eleven hundred more attend private schools.

The Board of Education is composed of eight members, elected by the voters of the city, and who hold office for the term of two years, without pay, and a city superintendent of schools, also elected, and who is ex-officio a member of the Board. The Board of Education has full and complete control of the public schools; and while the different boards have always been liberal in the payment of salaries to teachers—thus enabling them to secure the best talent; prudent in directing large and substantial buildings, and thoughtful in providing the best of furniture and conveniences,—they have never been charged with waste or extravagance.

The high school, with its five teachers, the peers of any in the state, an elegant building and costly scientific and mechanical apparatus, is the pardonable pride of our people, and, judged by its practical results, is second to none in the state of California. Pupils who enter it must pass a rigid examination in the studies prescribed in the grammar school course, and nearly all are graduates of the grammar schools. In this school a full three years' course of study is taught, and so thorough is the instruction given that the graduates enjoy the distinction of admission to any of the regular colleges of the State University of California without further examination. The course of study, it will thus be seen, embraces the requirements of a full academical course, including the languages, Latin, Greek, German and French, special attention being given to the German language, the study of which is commenced in the grammar schools.

The Sacramento Grammar School, an elegant brick building, three stories in height, containing sixteen class-rooms and a large hall for assembly purposes, is situated in the northern part of the city, while the Capital Grammar School, a new frame structure, costing about thirty thousand dollars, is situated in the southern part of the city, the two schools being so situated as to be within easy walk of all the pupils. The nine primary schools are situated at convenient intervals throughout the city, commencing at Fourth and Q streets, and the last being at Twenty-eighth and J streets.

The night school is situated at Tenth and I streets, in a building lately purchased by the department, and being almost in the heart of the city, is especially convenient to all who attend.

The cost of maintaining the public schools in Sacramento city, including all expenditures, has, during the last five years, averaged a little more than one hundred thousand dollars per annum—a munificent sum, expended for the most worthy of all objects.

The public schools of the county, outside of the city, are under the immediate supervision of boards of trustees, who, in turn, are directed by a county superintendent of schools.

Benjamin F. Howard, the present able county superintendent of schools, has kindly furnished the following data, which shows at a glance the healthy condition of the schools under his supervision:

Number of school houses in the county, including joint districts	68
Number of grammar schools	45
Number of primary schools	29
Number of new districts organized, 1886-7	2
Number of school houses built of brick	1

Number of school houses built of wood	67
Number of male teachers employed	21
Number of female teachers employed	53
Average monthly wages of male teachers	$70
Average monthly wages of female teachers	60
Number of certificates granted to male teachers	3
Number of certificates granted to female teachers	31
Number of applicants rejected	41
Number of census children between 5 and 17 years of age	2443
Average daily attendance	1387
Percentage of attendance on average number belonging	92
Number of high school pupils	34
Number of grammar grade	564
Number of primary grade	1382
Cash paid for teachers' salaries	$33,541 95
Cash paid for rents, repairs and contingent expenses	6,145 34
Cash paid for school libraries	2,354 84
Cash paid for school apparatus	361 83
Total current expenses for year	$42,403 96
Valuation of school property and furniture	72,743 00
Valuation of school libraries	15,647 00
Valuation of school apparatus	4,328 00
Total valuation of school property	$92,718 00

In addition to the complete educational system detailed above, Sacramento city is liberally provided with private educational institutions, both secular and sectarian, many of which have been successfully conducted through a long series of years, and have fairly earned the liberal support they receive from their patrons.

Most prominent among these institutions may be named the Sacramento Institute, a select day and boarding school for boys, with a corps of instructors consisting of a principal and ten professors; St. Joseph's Female Academy, a day and boarding school for girls, with a large faculty and upwards of two hundred and fifty pupils; the Young Ladies' Seminary, conducted by W. S. Hunt; Howe's Normal School, conducted by Prof. E. P. Howe, one of the most experienced and thorough teachers in the State; the Sacramento Home School, conducted by Mrs. F. M. Ross. The Sacramento Business College, conducted by Prof. E. C. Atkinson, was founded in 1873, and so thorough has been the instruction imparted that many of the business men of Sacramento city received their business education at this institution. Another business college has lately been started by Professor Bainbridge, which promises to be a success, intellectually and financially.

The above article has been written for the purpose of giving a correct idea of the condition of educational interests in the city and county of Sacramento. Believing that the chief glory of a people lies in educating the masses to a knowledge of their duties as citizens of a great nation, and their responsibilities as members of society, and that, through the medium of the common schools, this knowledge can be best imparted, the citizens of Sacramento city and county feel that they have done their full duty in this respect, and that nowhere are better facilities afforded for securing an education than in the capital city of the state.

Social and Fraternal Organizations.—In the city of Sacramento societies of the Masons and Odd Fellows have each imposing and costly temples, the upper stories being divided into halls, in which the meetings of the various lodges are held. About every fraternal society is represented in the city by one or more lodges. In the larger towns of the county numerous lodges exist and at many points the stronger societies own their hall buildings.

THE SANITARY ASPECT OF SACRAMENTO.
By JAMES H. PARKINSON, City Physician.

Sacramento, the capital of the state, is situated at the junction of the Sacramento and American rivers, in latitude 38° 35′, longitude 121° 30′; height above sea level 30 feet. The site is comparatively level, there being a slight fall of four inches to the block from north to south. The natural level has been raised by the official grade two to three feet in all parts of the city, while I, J and K streets have been raised ten to twelve feet for thirteen blocks, and L street for a portion of that distance. The soil is alluvial deposit, the site having been periodically overflowed at high water for ages. The city is now amply protected by levees so excellently constructed that but little sipage occurs during the highest water. The porous condition of the soil facilitates the rapid removal of surface water except during the brief periods when the river level is above that of the city. The alternate rise and fall of the river produces a flushing or suction action, whereby the subsoil is alternately filled with water and drained, thus largely purifying it. The level of the ground water varies with the character of the season and the time of year, being roughly from one to six feet, according to locality. The more densely populated parts of the city are well sewered, the matter passing by gravity flow through a canal outside the city limits into a chain of lakes some miles to the southward. During the season when the water level no longer admits of flow by gravity the sewage is discharged into a reservoir, and thence pumped into the river. The water supply of the city is derived from the Sacramento, and is pumped directly into the supply pipes without previous treatment. This water is of uniformly excellent quality; its appearance at certain seasons is characteristic of streams flowing through alluvial soil between soft banks periodically submerged. By proper filtration it can be perfectly cleared, and then makes a very agreeable table water. An analysis by Prof. Hilgard shows

		Grs.
Carbonate of soda	per gallon,	0.27
Chloride of sodium, sulphate of sodium	"	1.42
Carbonate of lime	"	0.31
Carbonate of magnesia	"	0.25
Silica	"	1.85
Sulphate of lime	"	0.42
Phosphate of lime	"	1.48
Iron and manganese carbonates	"	0.63
Alumina	"	0.07
Vegetable matter	"	0.00
Total	"	6.69

This equals the average drinking water in any locality.

The climatology of Sacramento bears a general resemblance to that of the great valley in which it lies, the mean annual temperature for the nine years ending 1886 being 60.2, the mean maximum and minimum being 82.5 and 41.4, giving a range of 41.1; extremes of temperature are absent, the winters being mild and the summers uniformly cool. This is perhaps best shown by the fact that in the nine years from 1878 to 1886 there have been only 96 days on which the temperature was below 32°, and but 331 days on which the mercury rose above 90°, giving an annual average of 10 and 37 days respectively. The great feature which renders the summer climate pleasurable is the universal prevalence of cool nights; the mean temperature of the nights from June to August, during the years 1877 to 1887, was 60.0, and there were only nineteen nights in which the thermometer stood at or over 70°. This fact is due to the trade wind which reaches us as a south breeze at about 4 P. M., and continues blowing with a mean summer velocity of seven miles till early morning. The numerous shade trees and liberal sprinkling of the streets in summer perceptibly lower the temperature during the days of extreme heat.

The seasons are divided distinctly into dry and wet. The latter comprises the months of November to May, the dry from June to October. The months of greatest precipitation are December and January. For the 37 years from 1850 to 1886, the maximum precipitation was 34.92, the minimum 8.44, giving a mean of 19.60. The mean relative humidity for the years 1879 to 1884 was 67.4, or 60.2 for the dry and 72.8 for the wet seasons.

The prevailing diseases are those of a malarial type. This is invariably of a mild form, the malignant ague of the southern and middle states being here of the rarest occurrence. Malaria is now much less prevalent than in former years, and shows a steady annual decline in the number of cases, as well as in the change from remittent and quotidian to the milder second and third day fevers. This change is due to improved drainage, the general elevation of the city level, and to the great increase in the amount of ground under cultivation. With the exception of malarial trouble there is no endemic disease in the Sacramento valley, and this prevalence is now due to the fact that throughout the county the greater portion of the rural population is located on the rich bottom lands of the Sacramento, American and Cosumnes rivers. Each season brings its quota of disease to which atmospheric conditions may predispose, but speaking generally it may be stated that owing to the milder climate the diseases of exposure are here less prevalent. In considering the subject of vital statistics, it must be borne in mind that in common with other centres of population Sacramento receives annually many invalids whose deaths ought not properly to be credited to the general mortality. This is particularly the case in connection with the railroad hospital, which receives during the year the sick and injured from all portions of California, as well as from other states. Notwithstanding the foregoing, the annual death rate compares most favorably with that of other cities. For the years from Nov. 1, 1885 to 1887, the mean annual rate per 1,000, on an estimated population of 30,000, was 13.05; the mean monthly death rate for the year 1886 was 13.20, and for the year 1887, 13.10. The mean annual mortality from zymotic diseases for 1886 and 1887 was 47.5; the mean monthly mortality being 3.95. The presence or absence of zymotic disease in a given locality may be taken as good evidence of its sanitary condition and as a reliable test of its salubrity; these figures, therefore, are self-evident testimony of the general healthfulness of Sacramento.

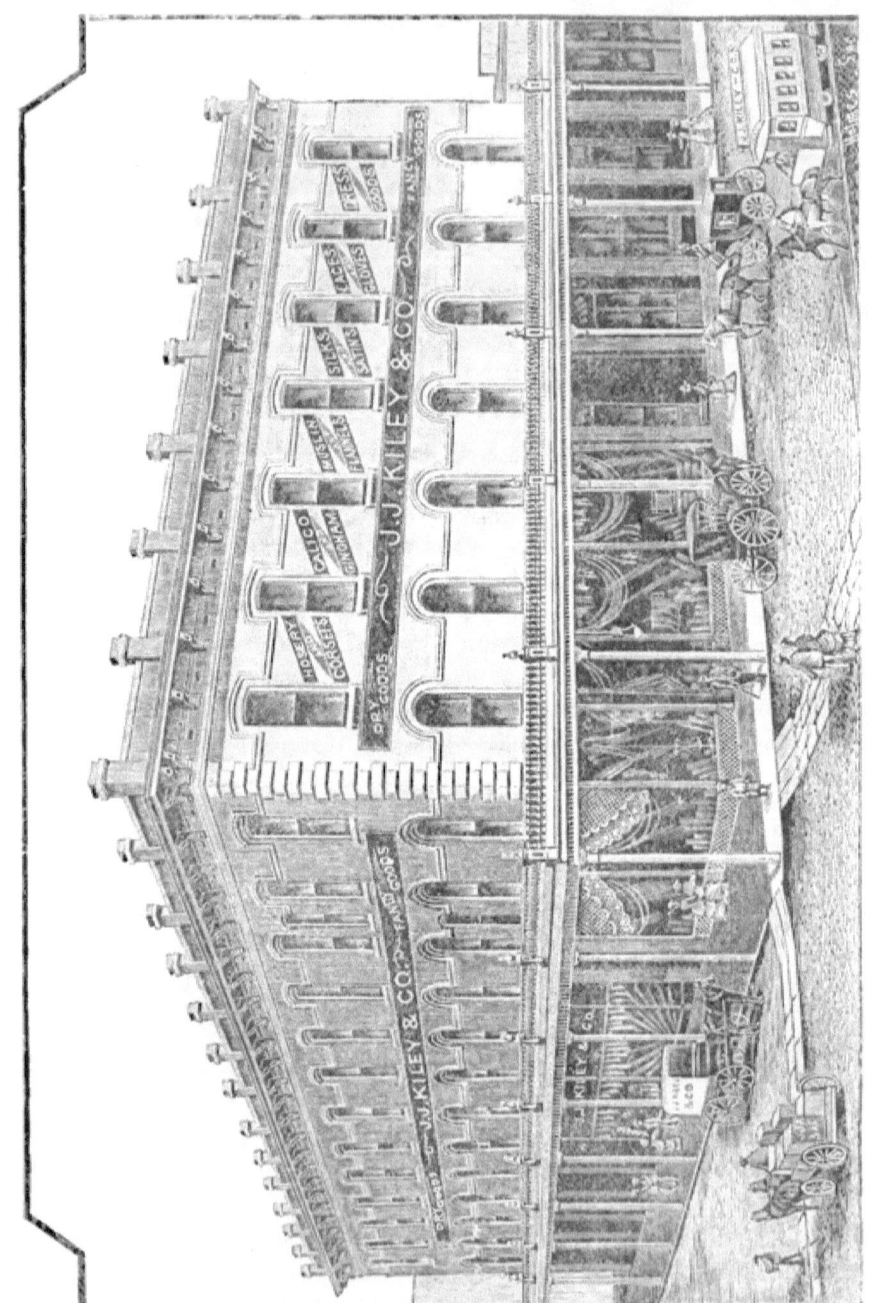

Clunie Building and Kiley's Dry Goods Store.

The opposite illustration is a representation of the Clunie building, on the northeast corner of Eighth and K streets. The building is owned by General Thomas J. Clunie, and the ground floor is occupied by the spacious dry goods store of J. J. Kiley & Co.

"Westward the Star of Empire Wends its Way."

In a few years more the population of California will become as dense as that of the eastern states and Europe. Sacramento city, the capital of the state, is also the headquarters of the great Sacramento valley and its adjacent surroundings, and has an area twice the size of any two of our eastern states and a soil and climate unexcelled if not superior to any other clime, producing almost any variety of vegetation grown in tropical and temperate climes. Railroads, with their ribs of steel, reach out from here in every direction to the farthest bounds of the Union, while the Sacramento river, with its 400 miles of navigation from the golden gate on the south to its headwaters on the north, gives us wonderful commercial advantages. Soon our city will claim a population of 100,000, and millions of tons will be freighted from here to all parts of the Union and to countries beyond the seas. This is the central point of the fruit producers of California, nine-tenths of which were forwarded from this city in 1887 to the east by rail, and over 400 cars of this number were forwarded by our house alone. We have been engaged in this branch of trade for many years, and are one of the largest shippers to eastern markets. We also own one of the largest and best nurseries in California, and can supply settlers who come here to make homes with any trees and other nursery stock that will be required at the lowest rates.

We are also owners and agents for many choice tracts of land that will be disposed of this season, and which are offered at great bargains, nearly all of which will double in value in a short time. In the list now offered for sale is :

"Orange Hill," 28 miles from Sacramento, on the overland railroad, at Penryn, Placer county, one-half mile from railroad depot. Fifty acres in full bearing and four acres in alfalfa. Orange, lemon, cherry, apricot, apples, peaches, etc., and a full variety of vines, now fast coming into full bearing. The proceeds of the crop of 1887 was over $4,000, and will doubtless be over $6,000 in 1888. Good comfortable dwelling house, barns, etc., and a splendid location. Sacramento capitol can be seen from the house. Price, $14,000; a great bargain.

"Olive Place." 120 acres, 28 miles from Sacramento, at Penryn, ¼ mile from depot, mostly planted and in cultivation with fruit trees and vines. Trees partly in bearing this year, and will all be in full bearing in two years. This place is planted with a view of cutting up into 10 and 20-acre tracts, with fine building spots, and a full variety of fruit trees on each tract. Price, if cut up, $135 per acre, or as a whole for $15,000.

50 acres choice land, one mile from city limits; house, barn and young vineyard. All fine orchard and vineyard land. $135 per acre; a bargain.

115 acres, on line of railroad and one quarter mile from city limits. This splendid property we are now using for nursery purposes, and have planted in fruit trees of the most desirable and best market varieties. We propose vacating it for nursery use, and about April or May will divide the property into half-acre to ten-acre plots, with fine avenues. A large portion of the

fruit trees will be in fine bearing condition the coming season. The best of water and in abundance on the ground. Railroad station near the ground; 10 minutes and 10-cent trips to city depot. This will make splendid suburban homes for those doing business in the city, and in the near future will double and quadruple in value.

We have 30 or more good city lots in the city at prices ranging from $300 and upwards.

Terms of payment on any of the above will be made satisfactory. Besides those named, we have quite a list of very desirable property adapted to fruit culture, for which we are at liberty to negotiate sales or direct purchasers. Correspondence solicited, and any information we can render will be cheerfully given. W. R. Strong & Co., Sacramento, Cal.

Hough's Magnetic and Mineral Springs.

Are situated in a romantic spot in Lake county—the Switzerland of California. They are on the road to and within three and seven miles respectively from the celebrated Allen springs and Bartlett springs. There are 240 acres in the property, of which quite a good proportion is tillable, and all supplies in shape of vegetables or fruit are grown on the property. The hotel contains 20 rooms. The stable accommodates 24 horses. There are also on the place a 5-room cottage and 9 cabins, a billiard hall, dance hall, blacksmith shop, bath house, a 2,500-gallon water tank, agricultural implements, hotel furniture, two horses, 6 head of stock, chickens, etc., and everything necessary for carrying on a health and summer resort. Postoffice and telegraph office in the hotel.

The character of the waters are tonic and laxative, and are very beneficial for stomach troubles. Their effect on dyspeptics is most wonderful. Patients who have suffered untold miseries and spent small fortunes in medical advice and medicines have been relieved almost immediately, and in a short time permanently cured by the use of the waters. All disorders of the kidneys and liver and malarial disorders are also permanently cured. Fish and game are abundant. The climate is unsurpassed, the thermometer ranging from 30° to 98°. As many of the guests are invalids, it would be a good investment for a physician. The altitude is 1,942 feet. Cache creek runs through the place, affording an abundance of pure cold water. The price for the 240 acres, with all the personal property, is only $15,000. A. Leonard & Son, real estate agents, 1014 Fourth street, Sacramento.

An illustration of the farm of Senator Joseph Routier, near Routier's station, on the line of the Sacramento valley railroad, about 10 miles from the city of Sacramento, appears in this volume. The farm is on the south bank of the American river, and consists of 222 acres, including some of the best bottom land in the county. It is in a high state of cultivation—100 acres being in vineyard and 100 in orchard—and none but the choicest varieties have been selected for planting. There are also a number of elegant orange trees. A specialty has been made of French prunes and almonds. No irrigation is required, as the natural percolation of water through the soil from the river affords all necessary moisture. The Senator settled there in June, 1853, and is one of the first successful fruit raisers and wine makers in the State. He has a winery of large capacity. Senator Routier has also made a specialty of fine stock raising. The view represents about fifty acres of the farm, as it appears looking to the north.

RESOURCES OF SACRAMENTO COUNTY.

WITHIN the last few years the fruit canning industry in this state has increased from a modest beginning to an importance which ranks it among the leading. The superiority of the fruit produced in the central portion of the state, in point of flavor and firmness above those produced elsewhere, peculiarly adapt it for preservation by the canning process. Keeping full pace with the advancement of our fruit interests, the Capital Packing Company's business has steadily increased. Located at Sacramento, in the midst of the finest fruit district in the state, they are in a position to secure the choicest of production. Their brands are established in the markets of the world, and carry with them the guarantee of excellence of the quality of the goods. The cannery employs a large force of women and children, and during the packing season considerable difficulty is experienced in procuring necessary help. During this season they have handled about 2,000 tons of fruit and vegetables, and in 1887 over 100,000 cases of goods were put up. These goods are mainly sent to the eastern states, but they have a ready market also in Europe, Japan and Australia, beside those sold for Pacific coast consumption. Their goods command a higher price in the market than those of any other cannery.

THE Pioneer Milling Company, H. G. Smith, president, Llewellyn Williams, vice-president, and F. B. Smith, secretary, conduct the oldest and largest flouring mills in Central California. The mills are located on the bank of the Sacramento river, and river steamers and barges receive and discharge at their wharf. A side track runs along the other side of the immense building affording unexcelled rail facilities. The mills are fully equipped with the latest improved roller process machinery, and have a capacity of 500 barrels per day. Their manufactures stand foremost in the market. The company deal largely also in grain of all kinds and mill feed.

JAMES SEADLER, ARCHITECT, SACRAMENTO.

Friend and Terry Lumber Company.

The Friend & Terry Lumber Company, the successor to the business of the pioneer lumber firm of Friend & Terry, carries on, at Sacramento and San Francisco, an extensive lumber business. At Sacramento the company has two extensive yards—at Second and M and at Thirteenth and J streets—and from them have been drawn the main materials which have been used in the construction of most of the wooden buildings in Sacramento and adjoining counties. Their prices for lumber are lower than those elsewhere in the state, and are fully 25 per cent. lower than those which are charged in the southern portion of the state. They deal in sugar pine, redwood, Oregon and Truckee pines, and carry besides a full line of fine finishing woods. Sacramento being the natural point for shipments of lumber products, the company enjoys a magnificent trade of wholesale as well as local. The company are interested in several mills in the lumber region, and have facilities and advantages in their line of business superior to those enjoyed by any other firm or company on the coast. The Sacramento business of the company is managed by E. J. Holt. W. E. Terry is president of the corporation.

BANK EXCHANGE BUILDING.

This building, located at the northwest corner of Second and K streets, and now owned by Angus Ross, is an excellent specimen of the architecture of the flush early days of Sacramento and the state. It was built at a time when, if business was prosperous, no expense was spared to erect a superb structure. Unlike many of the early-day favorites, its location has been such that it has kept full pace with the advancement of time, and it has always been and is now a particularly remunerative piece of property. Lately extensive improvements have been made on the building.

Enlarged! Refurnished! Renovated!
CAPITAL HOTEL,

Corner of Seventh and K Streets,
SACRAMENTO, CAL.

THE IDEAL TOURIST AND COMMERCIAL HOUSE
Of Central and Northern California.

Central Location.   Experienced Management.   Polite Attention.
BUSES AND HACKS OF THE HOUSE MEET ALL TRAINS.

☞ *FIRST CLASS.* ☜   *BLESSING & GUTHRIE, Proprietors.*

SIGN OF THE TOWN CLOCK.

H. WACHHORST,

Leading Jeweler of Sacramento

No. 315 J Street.

THE MOST ELEGANT ESTABLISHMENT
In this line between San Francisco and the Rockies.

DIAMONDS IN VARIETY,
AND OTHER PRECIOUS STONES,
WATCHES, CHRONOMETERS,
CLOCKS AT ALL PRICES,
RINGS, BROOCHES, PINS,
SILVERWARE, ETC.

At Wachhorst's Bijou Diamond Palace.

WE RECOMMEND

JOHN F. COOPER'S
Music Store

SACRAMENTO. - - - CALIFORNIA

For the Latest Sheet Music; Pianos and Organs Sold on the Installment Plan. Sole Wholesale and Retail Manufacturers' Agent for the

MATHUSHEK PIANOS.

Also, Ten Different Makes. ☞PIANOS TO RENT.

Everything in the Music Line.

Mrs. E. Katzenstein,

THE LEADING

MILLINER,

No. 605 J Street,   *Between Sixth and Seventh,*

SACRAMENTO, CAL.

Importer of Laces, Ribbons and Flowers.

LATEST PARISIAN FASHIONS,

Pattern Bonnets, beautiful in design, rich in material, and perfectly new.

Large assortment, in all colors, styles of trimmings, and to suit any age or complexion, in dress, riding, and traveling hats; garden, school, and evening hats.

ALL NEW STYLES RECEIVED IMMEDIATELY ON THEIR INTRODUCTION IN NEW YORK.

First-class Milliners employed in our trimming department, and all orders from at home or abroad will have special attention and a guarantee of satisfaction.

C. S. HOUGHTON,
WHOLESALE BOOKSELLER AND STATIONER.
→PUBLISHER OF←

CALIFORNIA FOR FRUIT-GROWERS AND CONSUMPTIVES. (Illustrated.) Price, $1.00, postpaid.

THE ORANGE, ITS CULTURE IN CALIFORNIA. (Illustrated.) Price, $1.00, postpaid.

615 J Street,   -   -   -   Sacramento, Cal.

─GOODS FOR ALL─
Needs, Tastes and Purposes.

THE most successful and growing stores in the country to-day are the large, complete and many-sided stores, with goods suited to all needs, tastes and purposes. Looked at from a single standpoint, they may seem too voluminous and complex; looked at from the standpoint of the multiform demands of the day, nothing less will suffice. There is no test like *experience* and *practical results*, and these support the complete stores.

Ours is the largest and most complete general outfitting establishment on the coast, as it is also the most successful. It has the largest trade, both at home and through the mails, and shows the most rapid growth; and its growth has been the most rapid just as its assortments were at their best and highest.

The key to its success is that it furnishes what the people—and all the people—want. It ministers to every demand. It is varied and all-embracing. All its customers may not buy in every department, perhaps, but every one finds what he looks for and is interested in. There are coarse, stout goods, for rough usage; plain, serviceable goods, for everyday wear, and fashionable and costly goods from Vienna, Paris, London and other market centers of the world. In each of these grades only the best makes are represented, while the prices are always as low, and in most cases lower than those of any other dealers.

Our MAIL ORDER DEPARTMENT is the largest on the coast, and in busy seasons we receive as high as eight hundred to one thousand orders per day. Our Illustrated Catalogue, giving prices and full descriptions of all our goods, is sent free to any address, together with any samples that may be desired.

Weinstock & Lubin

ONE PRICE.

Dry Goods, Clothing, Shoes, Hats, Millinery, Notions, Household Supplies, Etc.

Nos. 400, 402, 404, 406, 408 and 410 K Street,

SACRAMENTO, CAL.

UNION HOTEL,

ISADORE TOWNSEND, PROPRIETOR.

Second Street, between J and K, - , Sacramento, Cal.
(TWO AND A HALF BLOCKS FROM RAILROAD DEPOT).

The Home of Tourists and Commercial Men.

STRICTLY FIRST-CLASS.

Conducted on the European Plan.

NEWTON BOOTH.   C. T. WHEELER.

BOOTH & CO.

1009, 1011, 1013, 1015. 1017, 1019 Front Street, between J and K,

SACRAMENTO. CAL.

Wholesale Grocers,

→AND DEALERS IN←

PROVISIONS, WINES, TOBACCO and CIGARS.

THE HOUSE has been in business for thirty-eight years, and its proprietors claim that their experience has given them a thorough acquaintance with the wants of the trade and knowledge of the condition of the market, the quality of and value of goods. Their store and warerooms are larger than those of any similar establishment in the State—100 feet front by 150 feet deep—and being situated immediately opposite the railroad freight depot, and within half a block of the steamboat landing, give them superior advantages for receiving, handling and delivering goods.

Special attention is paid to shipping all articles in good order and condition, and there is no charge for drayage.

The house has superior facilities for buying. IT BUYS FOR CASH. It has business connections in San Francisco, an agent in New York, and correspondents in Chicago, St. Louis, Baltimore, Cincinnati and Omaha. It carries a large stock and, it is believed, a greater variety and more complete assortment than any other house in the same line of business in the State; and particular attention is given to filling orders for goods not in regular line of trade, at lowest rates.

→GOODS WILL BE SOLD TO DEALERS WHO ARE RELIABLE←

At the Smallest Possible Advance, and Satisfaction Guaranteed.

ORDERS FROM THE TRADE SOLICITED.

The house is more desirous to do a large business, with satisfaction to its customers, than to make large profits, and will endeavor to make its own interests identical with those who deal with it. Business men visiting Sacramento are invited to call and inspect what is claimed to be the best assorted stock and most complete establishment of the kind on the Coast.

WE IMPORT TEA DIRECT FROM CHINA AND JAPAN.

W. D. COMSTOCK,

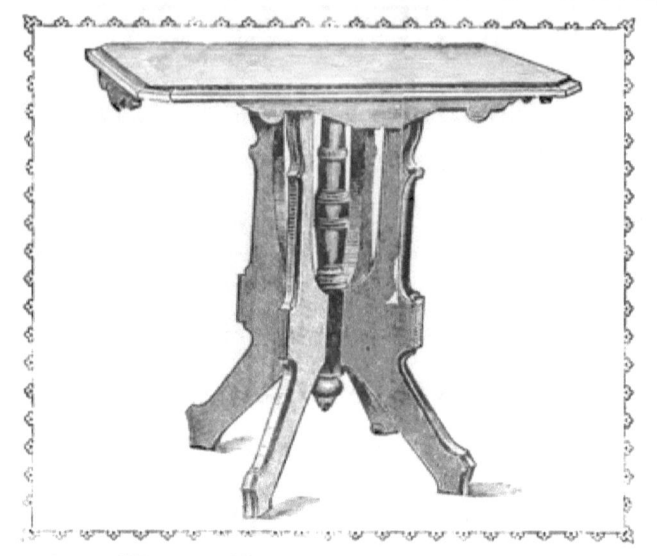

Furniture Warerooms, Corner Fifth and K Sts.

The Best Place for Bargains.

Newcastle Fruit Land For Sale

→BY←

ROBERT JONES,

Notary Public, Real Estate and Insurance Agent,

NEWCASTLE, PLACER COUNTY, CALIFORNIA.

NEWCASTLE, Placer County, is situated on the line of the Central Pacific Railroad, 32 miles from Sacramento, in the center of the Citrus Fruit Belt of Northern California. Fruit from this section has taken the first premiums at all the State and District Fairs; also, first premiums at Citrus Fair held in Sacramento December 12, 1886, for Oranges, Olives, Lemons and Raisins. Being at an altitude of 956 feet, the climate is unsurpassed in the State for all diseases of the throat and lungs. Unimproved land is selling at from $20 to $50 per acre; improved land, at from $150 to $300 per acre. Fruit ripens ten days earlier here than in any other section, and oranges ripen from five to seven weeks earlier than they do at Los Angeles or Riverside, thereby securing sure sale at a high price. There were over 350 carloads of fruit sent to the Eastern market from Newcastle this season, and at the rate they have been setting out orchards it will double that amount next season. People looking for cheap land and fine climate cannot find any better county in the State, as we have more advantages and fewer disadvantages than any other fruit-growing section in California.

I have a few tracts suitable for subdividing, which are well located as to roads and water, which I can offer very low. Also, some very fine improved farms, cheap. Any one looking for land, improved or unimproved, will do well to correspond with me, as I am well acquainted with this section of California.   ROBERT JONES.

→PHŒNIX FLOURING MILLS←

Corner Thirteenth and J Streets,

SACRAMENTO, CAL.

GEO. SCHROTH & CO.

Patent Roller Family Flour, Oat Meal, Buckwheat Cracked Wheat, Graham Flour, Ground Barley.

Agents for Cormack's Oat Meal and Nudavene Corn Meal.

These Mills have just been completed, and are operated on the FULL ROLLER SYSTEM. The Flour is ahead of any other in the market for whiteness and strength.

❖CAPITOL POTTERY❖

Corner Thirtieth and K Streets,

SACRAMENTO, CAL.

GEORGE MUDDOX, - - Proprietor.

This manufactory was established in 1879, with one man, and did a business the first year of $4,000. The business now amounts to $40,000 annually, and embraces the manufacture of

Pipes, Vases, Flower Pots, Fire Bricks and all kinds of Fire Clay.

Further improvements are now under way—including an entire set of new machinery, steam engine, etc—which will be completed by January 1, 1888.

→❖UNION BREWERY,❖←

JACOB GEBERT,
Proprietor.

20th and O Streets
SACRAMENTO.

UNION ❖ NURSERY,

Tenth Street, between U and V,

SACRAMENTO, - CALIFORNIA.

FRANK KUNZ,

FLORIST AND NURSERYMAN.

American ❖ Laundry,

CORNER NINETEENTH AND I STREETS,

Sacramento, Cal.

NO CHINESE EMPLOYED.

Office at Sawtelle's Book Store, 708 and 710 J Street.

E. H. GREEN, Proprietor.

ANDREW BOWMAN,
CARRIAGE PAINTER

417 Twelfth Street, between D and E,

SACRAMENTO, CAL.

N. W. ROBBINS,

No. 800 K Street, Southeast Corner Eighth,

SACRAMENTO.

CARRIAGE TRIMMING.

Cushions always on hand, and made at short notice.

GEO. SERMONET,

Wholesale and Retail Dealer in

Groceries and Provisions,

Corner of Eighth and G Streets,

SACRAMENTO, CAL.

A. INGRAM & CO.,

Carriages, Buggies, Spring Wagons.

REPAIRING A SPECIALTY.

Country orders promptly filled.

1013 and 1015 J Street, bet. 10th and 11th, Sacramento.

⁂THE BELL CONSERVATORY CO.⁂
SACRAMENTO, CALIFORNIA.

Horticulture!  **Floriculture!**

Dealers in Ornamental Trees and Shrubs, Garden, Greenhouse and Bedding Plants.

☞ THE GROWING OF FINE ROSES IS A SPECIALTY WITH US. ☜

We are direct importers of Holland and Japanese Bulbs. Olive and Fig Trees grown in quantity, and only the best varieties.

→ OUR FLORAL DEPARTMENT IS OUR SPECIAL PRIDE. ←

In the last two years we have received from the State Agricultural Society two gold medals and thirty-two premiums for excellence in Nursery Stock.

☞ All orders receive careful attention.

⁂NEW WM. TELL HOUSE⁂

Deutsches Gasthaus.

B. STEINAUER, Proprietor.

Board and Lodging, per week, · · · $5 00 to $7 00
Board and Lodging, per day, · · · · 1 00 to 1 25
Single Meals, · · · · · · 25 Cents.

☞ Families accommodated on reasonable terms.

NO CHINESE EVER EMPLOYED IN THE HOUSE.

The Bar is Well Stocked with Choice Liquors and Cigars.

814 and 816 J Street, between Eighth and Ninth,
SACRAMENTO, CAL.

PACIFIC HOTEL,

Corner Fifth and K Streets.

The Leading Business and Family Hotel of SACRAMENTO.

Board and Room, per day, $1 00, $1 25, $1 50
Board, per week, ... 4 00
MEALS, ... 25 CENTS.

Street Cars to and from the Depot pass the door every five minutes.

C. F. SINGLETON, Proprietor.

A. T. AMES,
Blacksmithing, Carriage Making,
HORSESHOEING and GENERAL JOBBING
GALT, CALIFORNIA.

HOME ✣ MADE ✣ BREAD.
MRS. M. KERLIN.   A. L. BOSCHKE.
KERLIN'S BAKERY,
Corner Tenth and F Sts., - Sacramento, Cal.

All kinds of Bread, Cakes, Pies, and Baked Beans, on hand and cooked to order.

We Carry the Largest Stock

—OF—   —AND—

BOOTS  SHOES

IN SACRAMENTO,

And therefore are able to fit any foot, from the very narrowest to the widest. OUR PRICES ARE THE LOWEST, QUALITY CONSIDERED.

GUS. LAVENSON, Corner Fifth and J Streets, Sacramento.

MISS A. E. VOTAW,
DEALER IN

FRENCH MILLINERY

CAREFUL ATTENTION
PAID TO
COUNTRY ORDERS.

No. 523 J STREET,
Bet. Fifth and Sixth,
SACRAMENTO, · · CAL.

➻ ALL THE LATEST NOVELTIES IN MILLINERY GOODS. ➺

J. BELLMER,
Dealer in
Groceries and Provisions,
WINES, LIQUORS, CIGARS, ETC.
☞ Goods delivered free of charge.
Corner M and Eighth Sts., Sacramento.

CANDY PARLOR.

GUS. HAGELSTEIN,
Manufacturer of
FINE CANDIES AND PURE ICE CREAM.
830 K STREET,
Corner of Ninth, SACRAMENTO.

L. P. ANDERSON,
HOUSE AND SIGN PAINTER,
816 K STREET,
Between Eighth and Ninth, - Sacramento.

J. E. PARMETER,
CARRIAGE + PAINTER,
916 and 918 Eleventh Street,
Between I and J, SACRAMENTO, CAL.
Prices to suit the times. Call and see me.

JOS. A. M. MARTIN,
—DEALER IN—

Mechanics' Tools, Etc.
920 J STREET,
OPPOSITE THE PLAZA, SACRAMENTO, CAL.

☞ AGENCY FOR IDEAL BICYCLES.

JAMES SEADLER,

MODERN ARCHITECTURE A SPECIALTY.

ORIGINAL DESIGNS for all kinds of buildings, and personal supervision given to construction.

Office and Residence, 627 J Street,

SACRAMENTO, CAL.

CAPITAL BOX FACTORY

TOWER BROS. & CO., PROPRIETORS,

Manufacturers of all kinds of

Fruit and Packing Boxes,

No. 1700 Second Street, Southwest Corner of Q,

SACRAMENTO, CAL.

JACOB GRIESEL,

Manufacturer of and Dealer in

SADDLES, Collars, HARNESS, Whips, Etc.

No. 1022 J STREET,

Between Tenth and Eleventh. SACRAMENTO.

R. WEBER,

St. Louis Market,

Corner of Eleventh and H Streets,

Sacramento.

All Kinds of Fresh Meats, Hams, Bacon, Lard, Sausages, Etc.

COLUMBUS BREWERY

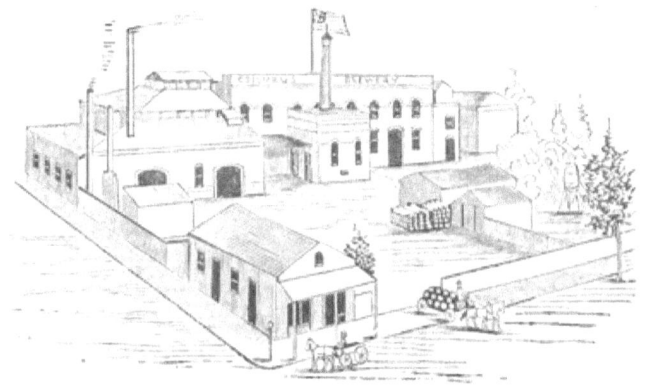

Corner of Sixteenth and K Streets, Sacramento, Cal.,

CHRISTOPHER WAHL, Proprietor.

The Columbus Brewery was established in 1852, with a brewing capacity of only eight hundred barrels yearly. Its present proprietor has $100,000 invested in the establishment, and has so enlarged the premises and increased the facilities as to bring the brewing capacity up to 20,000 barrels a year.

GALT AND ITS SURROUNDINGS.

A Flourishing Town Located in the Midst of a Rich Section of Country.

Few towns in the State have made the rapid and substantial advancement that has been achieved by the town of Galt in the few years that it has been in existence. It is located in the southern portion of the county, near the dividing line of San Joaquin County, on the line of the Western Pacific Railroad. From it a branch road extends to Ione, in Amador County. Its trade extends throughout the southern portion of the county, and to San Joaquin and Amador, and its business houses are large and extensive in their volume of trade. The soil of the surrounding section is rich and adapted to the production of cereals and all kinds of fruits and wines. A prominent citizen of the town writes, under date of November 26, 1887:

"I am engaged in diversified farming—grain raising, dairying (cheese making), and stock raising. I have also an orchard planted with nearly every variety of fruit, and the trees are all thrifty. I have also a small vineyard of the choicest varieties of table grapes. My grapes grow to the greatest perfection. I will add that neither my orchard nor vineyard have ever had a drop of water save that from rainfall, and I would not, from my experience, irrigate my lands for any purposes. The manufacture of raisins from the Muscat grape and the cultivation of the almond have been decidedly successful."

Land can be purchased in that section of the county at moderate prices; in the town, lots can be purchased reasonably, the payments to be made in installments.

NATIONAL BANK
—OF—
D. O. Mills & Co.
SACRAMENTO, CAL.

DIRECTORS:

EDGAR MILLS,	PRESIDENT.
S. PRENTISS SMITH,	VICE-PRESIDENT.
FRANK MILLER,	CASHIER.
CHAS. F. DILLMAN,	ASSISTANT CASHIER.

D. O. MILLS.

Sacramento Transfer Co.

Give your baggage check to our Messenger on train, and save your baggage from falling into irresponsible hands.

Baggage Delivered to all parts of the City, or STORED FREE OF CHARGE for one week, if passengers are undecided where to stop.

☞ BAGGAGE TAKEN ON STORAGE. ☜

Office, 530 K Street, Sacramento, Cal.   S. KINGSBURY & CO., Proprietors.

Barber & Pealer

IMPORTERS OF FINE FRENCH MILLINERY

621 and 623 J Street,

SACRAMENTO.

We carry the largest and finest stock of Millinery to be found in any retail store on the coast. Our mottoes are:

PROMPTNESS IN ALL BUSINESS TRANSACTIONS!

GOOD GOODS! LATEST STYLES! LOWEST PRICES!

AND EVERYTHING AS REPRESENTED!

CAREFUL ATTENTION GIVEN TO ALL COUNTRY ORDERS.

CARPET FACTORY,

802 M STREET, SACRAMENTO.

The Only First-class Carpet Factory in the City.

All Work Done, Guaranteed to Give Satisfaction.

MARY S. COWGER, Proprietor.

E. RILEY,

DEALER IN

Family Groceries,

HAY, GRAIN AND COUNTRY PRODUCE.

Corner Tenth and E Streets,   SACRAMENTO.

THE PIONEER DRUG STORE

OF SACRAMENTO.

—DEPOT FOR—

GOGING'S

CELEBRATED

FAMILY MEDICINES

904 J STREET.

NATIONAL GROCERY STORE

(WHOLESALE AND RETAIL.)

Choice Family Groceries, Provisions, Wines, Liquors, Tobaccos,

GRAIN, FLOUR AND GENERAL PRODUCE.

1028 and 1030 J Street, Southwest Corner of Eleventh,

SACRAMENTO, CAL.

Goods delivered free of charge to Steamboats, Railroad Depot, or any part of City.

CHRIS. EHMANN, Proprietor.

E. M. JUDGE & CO.

DEALERS IN

Groceries and Provisions,

WINES, LIQUORS, ETC.

Northeast Corner Twelfth and G Sts.

SACRAMENTO, CAL.

C. ZIMMERMAN,

DEALER IN

Groceries and Provisions

WOOD, HAY, GRAIN, WINES, LIQUORS AND CIGARS,

And Every Description of Family Supplies.

→ Goods Delivered Free of Charge. ←

Southeast Corner Twelfth and E Streets,

SACRAMENTO, CAL.

PLAZA HARNESS SHOP

Dealer in SADDLERY and HARNESS,

F. GEHRING, Proprietor,

912 J STREET. - - SACRAMENTO, CAL.

D. W. EILERS,

Wholesale and Retail Dealer in

Groceries and Provisions,

Southeast Corner Tenth and O Sts.

SACRAMENTO, CAL.

P. H. MENKEN'S,

928 J Street, - Sacramento,

IS THE

POPULAR EVENING RESORT FOR BUSINESS MEN

Pure Wines and Liquors and Fine Cigars. HOT LUNCH served daily, from 11 A. M. to 2 P. M.

W. F. NEUMAN,

Wagon and Carriage Manufacturer

→ HORSESHOEING. ←

Repairing of Wagons, Buggies, General Jobbing.

No. 1130 J Street.

Patronize Home Manufactures.

CAPITOL PACKING CO.

→ ESTABLISHED IN 1881 ←

Office and Works, Corner B and Eleventh Sts.,   SACRAMENTO, CAL

Over 2,000 Tons of Fruits Packed under our Famous Brands during 1887.

Bainbridge Business College

—AND—

NORMAL SCHOOL.

Short-hand, Type-writing, Music.

SELECT SCHOOL FOR BOTH SEXES.

920 and 922 K Street,
SACRAMENTO.

J. C. BAINBRIDGE, - - - PRINCIPAL.

PARK NURSERY

CORNER TENTH AND P STREETS,

F. A. EBEL, - - Proprietor.

Floral Designs a Specialty

J. H. MIDDLEMASS.   J. H. DOLAN.

DOLAN & MIDDLEMASS

Wholesale and Retail Dealers in

Groceries, Provisions, Produce,

CIGARS, TOBACCO, NOTIONS, ETC.

Northwest Corner of Seventh and N Streets,
SACRAMENTO.

Wilson's Stable,

318 K STREET,

Between Third and Fourth.   Nearly Opposite Postoffice,

SACRAMENTO, CAL.

Finest Turnouts in the City.

J. W. WILSON, Proprietor.

W. E. OSBORN,

No. 806 I Street, - - - Sacramento.

Agent Tahoe Ice Company

DEPOT FOR ALL KINDS OF FUEL.

Telephone No. 69.

L. ZOLLER,

M-Street Market,

Corner Eighth and M Streets.

Choice Fresh Meats, Hams, Bacon, Lard.

SADDLE ROCK

Restaurant and Oyster House.

➤➤FIRST-CLASS.◄◄

Ladies' Dining Room.

Open Day and Night.

The Leading Oyster House of Central California.

The finest Eastern and California Oysters, in every style. Game in season. Premium Steaks and Chops. Every variety of Fish.

1019 Second Street,

Between J and K,   SACRAMENTO, CAL.

Two and a half blocks from R. R. Depot.

P. ERAUW,

CASH GROCER

COR. EIGHTEENTH AND I STS.

SACRAMENTO.

Best Goods Sold at Lowest Prices

And delivered to any part of city free of charge.

A. LOTHHAMMER,

Sole Agent for STEINWAY & SONS, ERNEST GABLER & BRO., KRANICH & BACH, ROENISCH, and C. D. PEASE & CO.

PIANOS,
—AND—
WILCOX & WHITE ORGANS.

Piano Tuning and Repairing a Specialty.

1021 NINTH STREET,

Odd Fellows' Temple,   SACRAMENTO, CAL.

DAIRY.

PAUL WEISS,

Manufacturer of

Cheese, Butter, Etc.

2-Mile House,   Lower Marysville Road.

CAPITOL STORE.

WEBER & CO.
Wholesale and Retail Grocers
And COMMISSION MERCHANTS.

Highest quality, full weight goods, at the very lowest prices. Send for quotations and Price Current.

1217 and 1219 L Street,   **Sacramento, Cal.**

"*A Penny Saved is Equal to Two Earned.*"

PARK STORE,
JAMES POPERT, Proprietor,

Cor. Twenty-first and H Sts.   Sacramento.

Choice Family Groceries, Hay, Grain, Etc. Goods of the best quality at prices as low as any other store in the city.

S. DWYER,
Dealer in
Choice Family Groceries,
Provisions, Fresh Butter and Eggs
HAY AND GRAIN AT WHOLESALE AND RETAIL.
Corner Sixteenth and J Streets.

❄EUREKA MARKET❄
MORGAN & LUDLOW,
—DEALERS IN—

FRUIT,   **CHEESE**

Vegetables   AND

POULTRY,   General Produce

Butter

And Eggs.   **GAME** In Season.

1028 H Street,   Sacramento, Cal.

Louis Nicolaus,

CAPITAL BREWERY,

CORNER TWELFTH AND I STS.

SACRAMENTO,   CALIFORNIA.

[xvii]

MARTIN KESTLER,
Manufacturer of all kinds of Buggies,

FARM,

Express,

Freight,

Header

AND

Quartz

Wagons !

Constantly

on Hand

AND

MADE

TO

ORDER,

At Lowest Rates.

All Work Warranted.   Repairing Done at Short Notice.

1010, 1012 and 1014 NINTH STREET,

Between J and K.   SACRAMENTO, CAL.

P. G. RIEHL,

Dealer in Groceries, Provisions,

DRY GOODS,

Hardware, Crockery, Clothing, Boots and Shoes, Etc.

POSTOFFICE, FREEPORT, CALIFORNIA.

William Tell House,

Corner of Ninth and J Streets,

SACRAMENTO, CAL.

THE BEST FAMILY HOTEL IN SACRAMENTO.

MEALS, 25 CENTS.

Table supplied with the best the market affords. Accommodations first-class. Rates reasonable.

WM. NOETHIG, Proprietor.

(Late of San Francisco.)

METROPOLITAN MARKET

CONRAD SCHEPP,

Dealer in Fresh Meats

Of Every Description,

S.W. Corner Twelfth and E Streets,

SACRAMENTO.

LIVERY.

Farmers' Feed and Sale Stable,

J. D. LOCKHART, Proprietor,

Nos. 1015 and 1017 Eleventh Street,

Between J and K,   SACRAMENTO, CAL.

Horses boarded by the day, week or month. All kinds of Hay, Grain, Feed, Flour, and Potatoes.

I. M. SMITH & CO.

⇢⁕ G A L T ⁕⇠

Sacramento County, California,

HAVE FARMS

Of All Sizes and of Every Description,

FOR SALE ON EASY TERMS.

TOWN LOTS AND IMPROVED TOWN PROPERTY

At Prices and Terms to Suit All Purchasers.

Five and Ten Acre Tracts adjoining Town.

Intending purchasers will do well to correspond with this agency, or call and examine our bargains, before investing elsewhere. No trouble or charge to show property. Call on or address **I. M. SMITH & CO.,**
Galt, Sacramento Co., California.

J. H. FERRIS,

REAL ESTATE AGENT

GALT, SACRAMENTO COUNTY,

CALIFORNIA,

Has For Sale Parcels of the

Most Desirable Lands in the State,

In Tracts of from Four Thousand Acres down to Forty Acres. These Lands

PRODUCE IN GREAT ABUNDANCE

Hops, Corn, Alfalfa, Potatoes, and all kinds of Fruits and Vegetables, WITHOUT IRRIGATION, and Mr. Ferris is bound to satisfy every person seeking a home, or give them a free ride over one of the most interesting sections of California, which will pay for the trouble.

1060 acres of Hop, Alfalfa, Corn and Grass Land, on the side of the Cosumnes River, adjoining Arno Station, at $45 per acre.

840 acres, on the Lagoon—all in grain—at $40 per acre, including crop, or $30 per acre without the crop.

796 acres, near Galt; highly improved; $100 per acre.

3,500 acres, at Cicero Station; $30 per acre.

1,800 acres, on Dry Creek, 10 miles east of Galt; $40 per acre.

A Home Guaranteed to Every Man in Good Faith Seeking One.

J. H. FERRIS,

REAL ESTATE AGENT,

Office and Residence, Fourth Street, between A and B, Galt.

[xx]

JOHN HABERKORN,

MERCHANT TAILOR

ALWAYS ON HAND

A Large Assortment

OF THE

Latest and Best Goods,

BOTH

Foreign and Domestic.

LOWEST PRICES

Excellent

Workmanship

AND

A FIT GUARANTEED.

413 J Street, Sacramento, Cal.

CURTIS BROS. & CO.

WHOLESALE DEALERS IN

Fruit and Produce

308, 310 and 312 K STREET,

SACRAMENTO, CAL.

SHERMAN & PARKER,

Real Estate and Insurance Agents.

Property of all Descriptions

FOR SALE.

MONEY TO LOAN.   INSURANCE EFFECTED.

1007 Fourth Street.

SACRAMENTO, CAL.

Sacramento Planing Mill.

HARTWELL, HOTCHKISS & STALKER,

MANUFACTURERS OF

Doors and Windows, Blinds, Moldings, Etc., Etc.

Finish of all kinds, and Window and Door Frames.

STAIR WORK A Specialty

Brackets, Scroll-Sawing, Turning

CORNER FRONT AND Q STREETS,

SACRAMENTO, CAL.

A. & A. HEILBRON,

—DEALERS IN—

HARDWARE AND AGRICULTURAL IMPLEMENTS

217 and 219 J Street, Sacramento, Cal.

We keep a Full Stock of the following:

Caldwell & Olds Farm Wagons.
Casaday and San Leandro Gang Plows.
Vineyard and Side-hill Plows.
LaDow Disc Harrows.
Victor and Crown Mowers.
Hodge Case Headers.
Glidden Barb Wire.

Oliver Chill and Peoria Steel Plows.
Casaday and Peoria Sulky Plows.
Iron and Wood Frame Harrows.
Ajax and Planet Jr. Cultivators.
McCormack Binders.
Reindeer Rakes.
Perry Pleasure Carts, etc.

We also carry a complete assortment of Shelf and Heavy Hardware, including Nails, Rope, Iron, Steel, Coal, Shot, Powder, Fuse, etc.

Write Us for Prices!   Write Us for Prices!

"THE MELVILLE"

Formerly
THE TRUESDELL
1104
Market Street,
JUNCTION OF
MASON AND TURK
SAN FRANCISCO.

The leading family hotel of San Francisco. It is centrally located, thoroughly ventilated, with fine, airy, and sunny rooms, and is near to all the places of amusement. The table is excellent, the food and viands being the best obtainable.

Terms Reasonable. All Market Street Cars pass the main entrance.
ELEVATOR.

Hermann & Regensburger,
Proprietors.

WASHBURN & SCOTT,

Real Estate and Insurance Agents,

317 J Street, Sacramento, Cal.

H AVE FOR SALE lands suitable for the production of wheat and fruits of all kinds—including the orange, olive and fig—in small tracts, for man and family, and larger tracts, for colonies. Prices within reach of all. These lands are situated in Central and Northern California,

The Garden of the State.

GRAND CLIMATE.
BEAUTIFUL HOMES.
LOVELY SCENERY.

A. S. HOPKINS & BRO.

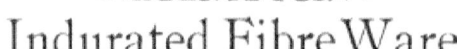

Importers of and Wholesale Dealers in

Wooden and Willow Ware,

311 and 313 J Street, between Third and Fourth, Sacramento.

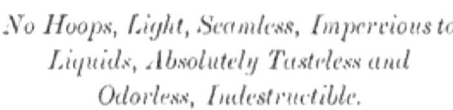

AGENTS FOR

Indurated Fibre Ware

No Hoops, Light, Seamless, Impervious to Liquids, Absolutely Tasteless and Odorless, Indestructible.

It is molded or pressed out in one piece from wood fibre saturated with a hardening material which makes it very durable as well as elastic, and renders it impervious to moisture, hot or cold. It is superior to wood, paper, tin and iron ware in these particulars. It will not shrink or swell; will not taint water, milk or other liquids; cannot leak, water-soak or rust; has no paint or varnish to wear off; does not require paint or varnish to preserve it; is proof against hot and cold water, kerosene, benzine and naphtha. It commends itself for general house and farm use; invaluable for manufacturers, brewers, malsters and paper makers; indispensable for steamer use, as, in addition to above qualities, the ware will not sink if dropped overboard.

Where's Your Merit?

Southern Boomer: "I'll sell you this corner lot for five hundred dollars a front foot."

Eastern Capitalist: "But, my dear sir, why pay five hundred dollars per front foot when I can buy good property in Northern California for half the price?"

Southern Boomer: "Ah! but where's your boom?"

The close-buying householder says to the thrifty grocer, "Why pay sixteen cents per pound for Our Taste Hams when I can buy others for a considerable less?" The thrifty and sensible grocer replies: "Ah! but where's your merit?"

There are no hams equal to the Our Taste—special cure and trim, taken from selected hogs, and imported from the East in refrigerator cars in sweet pickle.

All first-class grocers keep them.

HALL, LUHRS & CO., Proprietors.
Sacramento and Los Angeles.

L. L. LEWIS & CO.

502 and 504 J St. and 1009 Fifth St.

SACRAMENTO, CAL.

Ours is one of the largest Stove and Crockery Houses on the Pacific Coast. We keep everything that is necessary to fit out a family for housekeeping, and at Wholesale Prices. We sell our No. 7 Eclipse Stove for $10, and we warrant it to be a first-class baker and good cook stove in every particular.

We have beautiful Colored Tea Sets, of 44 pieces, at

$3.50.

This is a big bargain. Send for our Catalogue of Crockery, Glassware, Stoves and Ranges, Silver Plated Ware, Copper and Tinware. Our Catalogue is most complete, and is sent FREE on application.

L. L. LEWIS & CO.

502 and 504 J Street and 1009 Fifth St.

SACRAMENTO.

CALIFORNIA STATE BANK

Does a General Banking Business.

Draws Exchange on all the Principal Cities of the World.

OFFICERS:

PRESIDENT,	N. D. RIDEOUT
VICE-PRESIDENT,	FRED'K COX
CASHIER,	A. ABBOTT

DIRECTORS:

C. W. CLARK,	GEO. C. PERKINS.
JOSEPH STEFFENS,	J. R. WATSON,
N. D. RIDEOUT,	FRED'K COX,
A. ABBOTT.	

ESTABLISHED 1852
PIONEER MILLING CO.

(LOCATED AT SACRAMENTO AND YOLO BRIDGE.)

SACRAMENTO, - - CALIFORNIA.

Manufacturers of NEW PROCESS

CHOICE BAKERS' AND FAMILY FLOUR,

AND

DEALERS IN GRAIN AND MILL FEED.

Capacity, - 500 Barrels per Diem.

The manufactures of this establishment occupy the foremost position in the market, and are regarded with marked favor by merchants and consumers.

Cash Paid for all kinds of Grain.

SMITH & MUIR PLUMBERS

A FULL STOCK OF

GAS FIXTURES

LAMPS, GLOBES, ETC.

No. 412 J Street,

TELEPHONE 143.   SACRAMENTO.

COUNTRY ORDERS WILL BE PROMPTLY ATTENDED TO

H. J. GOETHE,
Real ✦ Estate ✦ Agent,
NOTARY PUBLIC AND CONVEYANCER,
1011 FOURTH STREET,   SACRAMENTO, CAL.

Deeds, Mortgages, Wills, Bills of Sale, Leases, Contracts, and all other documents, in English or German, promptly and carefully executed.

Agent of the North German Lloyd Steamship Company.

MONEY TO LOAN.

FOR FINE HATS
GO TO
J. F. SLATER
SUCCESSOR TO
J. C. MEUSSDORFFER
402 J ST
SACRAMENTO

HOLBROOK, MERRILL & STETSON,

—— IMPORTERS OF ——

Stoves and Metals,

PLUMBERS' GOODS, TINNERS' TOOLS AND MACHINES,

TINNERS' STOCK.

Tin Ware and House Furnishing Hardware,

IRON AND LEAD PIPE.

Force and Lift Pumps,

ETC.........ETC.........ETC.

Nos. 221 and 223 J Street,   Sacramento, Cal.

Crouch and Lyman
GAS FIXTURES.
PLUMBERS
511 J Street, Sacramento. Telephone 94

M. S. HAMMER

DRUGGIST AND APOTHECARY

N.E. Cor. Fourth and K Sts.
Opposite Postoffice.

CARL STROBEL,

NO. 321 J STREET, SACRAMENTO, CAL.

BARGAINS IN CITY PROPERTY, AND SMALL FARMS

Adjoining and Near Sacramento,

As well as land of every description and answering all kinds of agricultural pursuits.

BUSINESS CHANCES

Also will be found by calling on CARL STROBEL, Real Estate and Insurance Agent.

DR. H. H. PIERSON,

ARTIFICIAL TEETH,   DENTIST.   All Qualities and Prices.

Pure Nitrus Oxide Gas administered for the Painless Extraction of Teeth.
Correcting Irregularities of Children's Teeth a specialty.

DENTAL ROOMS: NO. 511 J STREET, SACRAMENTO, CAL.

FRED. KOLLIKER,

Southwest Corner Sixth and J Streets,   Sacramento, Cal.

Druggist and Pharmacist

— ALSO —

Sacramento Dental Depot.

ED. M. MARTIN,

Attorney at Law,

And NOTARY PUBLIC.

Office and Residence—No. 603 I Street, near corner of Sixth (almost adjoining the Hall of Records and Court House), Sacramento, Cal.

W. A. ANDERSON,

Attorney and Counselor

SACRAMENTO, CAL.

Office—No. 209 J Street (east of Wells, Fargo & Co.'s Express), Room No. 4.

CHAUNCEY H. DUNN,

Attorney at Law,

920 FIFTH STREET,

P. O. Box 372.   SACRAMENTO, CAL.

J. C. TUBBS,

Attorney at Law,

NO. 601 I STREET,

Corner of Sixth.   SACRAMENTO, CAL.

JOHN SHANNON,

Attorney at Law

And NOTARY PUBLIC,

626 I Street (Opposite Court House), Sacramento

EUGENE J. GREGORY.   FRANK GREGORY

GREGORY BROS. CO.

(Successors to GREGORY, BARNES & CO.)

WHOLESALE DEALERS IN PRODUCE AND FRUIT

Nos. 126 and 128 J Street, Sacramento, Cal.

Full stock of Potatoes, Vegetables, Green and Dried Fruits, Beans, Alfalfa, Butter, Eggs, Cheese, Poultry, etc., always on hand.
Orders filled at lowest rates.

PEOPLE'S SAVINGS BANK.

WM. BECKMAN..........President | WM. JOHNSTON.....Vice-President
WM. F. HUNTOON..Cashier

Capital Paid Up,   -   -   - $225,000.
Surplus Fund,   -   -   -   40,000.

Interest Paid on Deposits Semi-Annually.   Money Loaned on Real Estate Only.

Directors—Wm. Beckman, E. J. Croly, Wm. Johnston, E. C. Atkinson, John L. Huntoon, Geo. M. Hayton, Samuel Gottleib.

Office, Southeast Corner Fourth and J Streets, Sacramento, Cal.

[xxxi]

MECHANICS' ✦ EXCHANGE.

(Nearest Hotel to the Railroad Depot.)

Deutsches Gasthaus.

No. 120 I Street, between Front and Second,
SACRAMENTO, CAL.

Meals, · · · · 25 Cents | Beds, · · · · · · 25 Cents

JACOB SCHMID, Proprietor.

JAMES LONGSHORE,
SACRAMENTO TRUNK FACTORY
530 K STREET.

Masonic Building,   Sacramento, Cal.

Every description of

Trunks and Valises

Kept in Stock, Manufactured to Order and Repaired

The Only French Restaurant in Sacramento.

RESTAURANT DE FRANCE,
427 K STREET,

Adjoining Metropolitan Theater Building.

Entrance to Private Rooms on Fifth Street,

LOUIS PAYEN, Proprietor.

J. CARLAW.   A. CARLAW.

CARLAW BROS.
SACRAMENTO
Granite and Marble Works
CORNER TENTH AND R STREETS.

Quarriers and manufacturers of all kinds of Granite and Marble Work, and direct importers of the celebrated Scotch Granite Monuments.

See our work and get prices before purchasing elsewhere.

Central Restaurant
NO. 710 K STREET,
Bet. Seventh and Eighth,   Opposite Site of New Postoffice,

SACRAMENTO, CAL.

Coffee and Cakes, · · · · · · 10 Cents.
Meals, · · · · · · · · · 25 Cents.

Served at all hours.

Your Patronage is Invited. Please Call.

MRS. H. SCHINDLER, · PROPRIETRESS.

GRAND HOTEL BLOCK
Corner of Front and K Streets,
SACRAMENTO.

This house has been thoroughly renovated and newly furnished. It contains 16 rooms, and the location is one of the most desirable in the city, being opposite the steamer landing and in the midst of the wholesale mercantile quarter.

PRICES REASONABLE.

MRS. DRAKE, Proprietress.

A Gold and Ten Silver Medals Awarded by the California State Agricultural Society

F. FOSTER.   J. O. FUNSTON.

F. FOSTER & CO.

Book Binders,

PAPER RULERS,

· AND ·

Blank Book Manufacturers

No. 319 J Street, between Third and Fourth,

SACRAMENTO, CAL.

Resources of California Photography is forcibly exemplified by a visit to

Swasey's

GALLERY, No. 26 Montgomery Street
opposite the Lick House, San Francisco, Cal.
☞ Take the Elevator.

W. E. DOAN.   E. B. WILLIS.   W. J. DAVIS.

DAVIS, WILLIS & DOAN,

SHORT-HAND REPORTERS,

THE BEST SHORT-HAND FACILITIES

Of any office outside of San Francisco. Orders for all kinds of short-hand work and type-writing promptly attended to, and accuracy guaranteed.

OFFICE: COURT HOUSE, SACRAMENTO.

F. F. Gebbets

DENTIST,

No. 914 Sixth Street,   Between I and J,

OPPOSITE CONGREGATIONAL CHURCH.

SACRAMENTO.   CALIFORNIA.

S. J. JACKSON,

DEALER IN

STOVES AND RANGES

SHEET-IRON, TIN-WARE, ETC.

427 J Street, bet. 4th and 5th, Sacramento.

A FULL LINE OF OIL STOVES.

The Pioneer Stove Store in Sacramento. The prices are the lowest, and the stock most carefully selected.

Stanton, Thomson & Co.

308, 310 and 312 J Street, Sacramento.

→ SOLE AGENTS FOR ←

IMPERIAL PLOWS

The Best General Purpose Plows in the Market.

— ALSO, —

Mitchell & Lewis Co.'s Farm and Spring Wagons,
Corbin Disc Harrows,
Myers Force and Lift Pumps,
The Star Wind Mills,

And a full line of the most approved Farm Machinery.

Prescriptions Accurately Compounded at All Hours of the Day or Night.

J. C. SEPULVEDA,

DRUGGIST

Northeast corner K and Second Streets, and

BOSTON DRUG STORE,

Northeast corner Third and J Streets,   Sacramento, California.

EBNER BROS.	→ DEUTCHES GASTHAUS. ←
	EBNER'S HOTEL
WHOLESALE	CHARLES DIETRICH, Proprietor.
LIQUOR DEALERS	MEALS, . . 25 CENTS.
116 and 118 K Street,	Nos. 116 and 118 K Street.
	Between Front and Second, but half a block from Steamboat Landing and near Railroad Depot.
SACRAMENTO, . . . CALIFORNIA.	SACRAMENTO.

BAKER & HAMILTON,

—IMPORTERS AND MANUFACTURERS OF—

Agricultural Implements and Machines, Wagons, Carriages, Carts, BUGGIES, ETC.

No. 34.

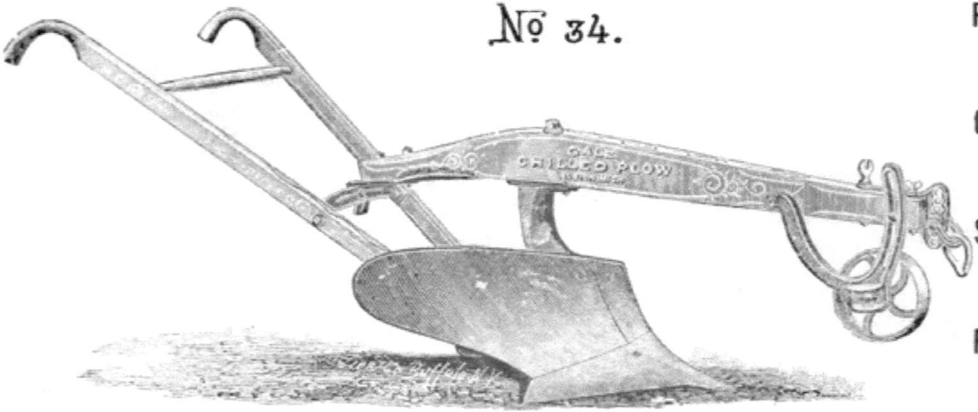

Headers,
Thresheres,
Combined
Harvesters,
Steam Engines,
Mowers,
Rakes,
Etc., Etc.

Plows,
Gang Plows,
Cultivators,
Harrows,
Seed Sowers,
Seed Drills,
Fan Mills,
Etc., Etc.

→DEALERS IN←

Barb Wire, Belting, Rope and Cordage, Cutlery, Powder, Guns, Cartridges, Shot, Iron, Steel, Coal, HARDWARE.

Address SACRAMENTO or SAN FRANCISCO. For Prices.

[xxxv]

WATERHOUSE & LESTER,

709, 711, 713 and 715 J Street, Sacramento,

→→IMPORTERS←←

HARDWOOD LUMBER AND CARRIAGE MATERIAL

Malleables for all Styles of Wagons and Carriages.

SPRINGS AND AXLES.

→→ALL GRADES OF←←

Buggy and Wagon Tops, Carriage and Wagon Umbrellas.

MANUFACTURERS OF

WAGON AND BUGGY BODIES,
ALL STYLES GEARINGS,
WOOD HUB WHEELS,
SARVEN PATENT WHEELS,
GENERAL JOB MILL WORK.

Waterhouse & Lester: New York, San Francisco, Sacramento, and Portland, Or.

The Largest and Best Equipped Printing House in Northern California.

W. J. HASSETT.   A. J. JOHNSTON.

A. J. JOHNSTON & CO.   SUCCESSORS TO   LEWIS & JOHNSTON,

BOOK AND JOB PRINTERS,

410 J STREET,   SACRAMENTO.

Orders from the Country

Are respectfully solicited, which will be promptly filled at reasonable prices.

[xxxvii]

JOSEPH HAHN & CO.

Corner Fifth and J Streets, Sacramento, Cal.

Wholesale Druggists.

TO THE TRADE.

We have constantly on hand a large and varied stock of Drugs, Chemicals and Patent Medicines. Proprietors of Hahn's Liver Bitters and Condition Powders. Sole agents for Dr. Kale's Rheumatic Remedy. Full line of Wythe & Bro.'s Preparations. An extensive assortment of Surgical Instruments. Large and choice stock of Wines and Liquors, both in cases and bulk; French Cognac and California Brandy; California Port, Sherry, Reisling and Burgundy; Blue Grass, Nabob, Bel Air and Dew Drop, in cases. Depot for the celebrated California Bartlett and Saratoga High Rock Spring Waters, in barrels and cases.

Very truly yours, JOSEPH HAHN & CO.

KLUNE & FLOBERG,

JEWELERS

428 J Street, Southwest Corner of Fifth,

SACRAMENTO, CAL.

HEADQUARTERS FOR FINE

Diamonds, Watches, Jewelry, Silverware, Optical Goods, Etc.

AGENTS FOR

ROCKFORD  **WATCHES**

are *unequalled* in exacting service. Used by the Chief Mechanician of the U. S. Coast Survey; by the Admiral Commanding in the U. S. Naval Observatory, for Astronomical work; and by Locomotive Engineers, Conductors and Railway men.

They are recognized as **THE BEST** for all uses in which close time and durability are requisites. Sold in principal cities and towns by the COMPANY'S Exclusive Agents (leading jewelers), who give a FULL warranty

W. E. TERRY, President   E. J. HOLT, Manager.

ESTABLISHED 1853

FRIEND & TERRY LUMBER CO.

REDWOOD,

Sugar, Oregon and Truckee Pine

AT WHOLESALE AND RETAIL,

And Manufactured to Order at Mills of the Company.

— ALSO —

SHAKES,   WINDOWS,

     BOLTS,   BLINDS,

        TIES,   SCREENS,

          DOORS,   ETC, ETC.

Main Yard and Office: - - - No. 1310 Second Street, near M.

Branch Yard: - - - - - Corner of Twelfth and J Streets.

SACRAMENTO, CAL.

Country Branch, - - - - - - - - Galt, California.

ORDERS BY MAIL PROMPTLY AND ACCURATELY FILLED.

The best facilities for shipping car-load lots direct from San Francisco.

W. R. STRONG & CO.

WHOLESALE FRUIT AND

PRODUCE MERCHANTS

PACKERS and FORWARDERS

In Carload Lots, to Eastern, Southern and Interior Markets.

Having been engaged in this business for many years, and being the oldest house and largest shippers on the Pacific Coast, our advantages are unrivaled for the disposal of California Fruits and Products in the great marts of their consumption.

Our arrangements with the leading Fruit and Produce Growers are very extensive, and we know we can be of the largest advantage to both the producer and consumer.

We keep constantly on hand, in their season, a

FULL STOCK OF TROPICAL FRUITS

As well as of California Growth. Also,

Canned Goods, Machine and Sun Dried Fruits, Butter, Cheese, Nuts, Etc.

CAPITAL NURSERIES,

W. R. STRONG & CO., Proprietors,

A FULL AND COMPLETE STOCK OF

Fruit, Shade and Ornamental Trees

SHRUBBERY, VINES, PLANTS, ETC.

SEED STORE AND PRINCIPAL OFFICE:

FRONT and J STREETS,   **SACRAMENTO, CAL.**

Main Depot and Sales Yard—Second Street, near Passenger Depot of C. P. R. R. extending across the block to Third Street.

Nursery Grounds—130 acres just outside the city limits, near County Hospital, and 60 acres near Penryn, Placer County, Cal.

By fair dealing and close attention to the wants of our customers, we are determined to merit the confidence of the public in the future, as we believe we have in the past.

W. R. STRONG & CO., Sacramento, Cal.

CAPITAL HAMS

We guarantee the Capital Ham to be unexcelled. We stop for neither price nor pains in getting Perfection in QUALITY, CUT and CURE.

LINDLEY & CO.

Wholesale Grocers,

SACRAMENTO,   CALIFORNIA.

HUNTINGTON, HOPKINS & CO.

DEALERS IN

General Hardware,

IRON, STEEL and COAL

And Blacksmiths' Supplies of Every Description.

WE CONSTANTLY CARRY IN STOCK A FULL LINE OF SHELF HARDWARE, AND BUILDING SUPPLIES OF ALL KINDS.

HEADQUARTERS FOR

Sportman's Supplies, Ammunition, Fishing Tackle,

WINCHESTER, MARLIN and BALLARD RIFLES.
PARKER, SMITH, and ENGLISH SHOT GUNS.

CUTLERY, Etc., Etc.

<u>PAINTED</u> **BARB WIRE** <u>GALVANIZED</u>

STEEL HAY AND BARLEY FORKS,

HOES, RAKES, SCYTHES, Etc., Etc.

WRITE FOR CATALOGUE AND PRICES.

𝔖acramento.

www.ingramcontent.com/pod-product-compliance
Lightning Source LLC
Chambersburg PA
CBHW030403170426
43202CB00010B/1475